Workshop for NLP Open Source Software 2018

Held at ACL 2018

Melbourne, Australia
20 July 2018

ISBN: 978-1-5108-6712-3

Printed from e-media with permission by:

Curran Associates, Inc.
57 Morehouse Lane
Red Hook, NY 12571

Some format issues inherent in the e-media version may also appear in this print version.

Printed by Curran Associates, Inc. (2018)

For permission requests, please contact the Association for Computational Linguistics at the address below.

Association for Computational Linguistics
209 N. Eighth Street
Stroudsburg, Pennsylvania 18360

Phone: 1-570-476-8006
Fax: 1-570-476-0860

acl@aclweb.org

Additional copies of this publication are available from:

Curran Associates, Inc.
57 Morehouse Lane
Red Hook, NY 12571 USA
Phone: 845-758-0400
Fax: 845-758-2633
Email: curran@proceedings.com
Web: www.proceedings.com

ACL 2018

NLP Open Source Software (NLP-OSS)

Proceedings of the Workshop

July 20, 2018
Melbourne, Australia

Gold Sponsors

NYU | Center for Data Science

kaggle

Silver Sponsors

NAVER

Google

Bronze Sponsors

zendesk

Introduction

With great scientific breakthrough comes solid engineering and open communities. The Natural Language Processing (NLP) community has benefited greatly from the open culture in sharing knowledge, data, and software. The primary objective of this workshop is to further the sharing of insights on the engineering and community aspects of creating, developing, and maintaining NLP open source software (OSS) which we seldom talk about in scientific publications. Our secondary goal is to promote synergies between different open source projects and encourage cross-software collaborations and comparisons.

We refer to Natural Language Processing OSS as an umbrella term that not only covers traditional syntactic, semantic, phonetic, and pragmatic applications; we extend the definition to include task-specific applications (e.g., machine translation, information retrieval, question-answering systems), low-level string processing that contains valid linguistic information (e.g. Unicode creation for new languages, language-based character set definitions) and machine learning/artificial intelligence frameworks with functionalities focusing on text applications.

There are many workshops focusing open language resource/annotation creation and curation (e.g. BUCC, GWN, LAW, LOD, WAC). Moreover, we have the flagship LREC conference dedicated to linguistic resources. However, the engineering aspects of NLP OSS is overlooked and under-discussed within the community. There are open source conferences and venues (such as FOSDEM, OSCON, Open Source Summit) where discussions range from operating system kernels to air traffic control hardware but the representation of NLP related presentations is limited. In the Machine Learning (ML) field, the Journal of Machine Learning Research - Machine Learning Open Source Software (JMLR-MLOSS) is a forum for discussions and dissemination of ML OSS topics. We envision that the Workshop for NLP-OSS becomes a similar avenue for NLP OSS discussions.

To our best knowledge, this is the first workshop proposal in the recent years that focuses more on the building aspect of NLP and less on scientific novelty or state-of-art development. A decade ago, there was the SETQA-NLP (Software Engineering, Testing, and Quality Assurance for Natural Language Processing) workshop that raised awareness of the need for good software engineering practices in NLP. In the earlier days of NLP, linguistic software was often monolithic and the learning curve to install, use, and extend the tools was steep and frustrating. More often than not, NLP OSS developers/users interact in siloed communities within the ecologies of their respective projects. In addition to engineering aspects of NLP software, the open source movement has brought a community aspect that we often overlook in building impactful NLP technologies.

An example of precious OSS knowledge comes from SpaCy developer Montani (2017), who shared her thoughts and challenges of maintaining commercial NLP OSS, such as handling open issues on the issue tracker, model release and packaging strategy and monetizing NLP OSS for sustainability.[1]

Řehůřek (2017) shared another example of insightful discussion on bridging the gap between the gap between academia and industry through creating open source and student incubation programs. Řehůřek discussed the need to look beyond the publish-or-perish culture to avoid the brittle "mummy effect" in SOTA research code/techniques.[2]

We hope that the NLP-OSS workshop becomes the intellectual forum to collate various open source knowledge beyond the scientific contribution, announce new software/features, promote the open source culture and best practices that go beyond the conferences.

[1] https://ines.io/blog/spacy-commercial-open-source-nlp

[2] https://rare-technologies.com/mummy-effect-bridging-gap-between-academia-industry/

Organizers:

Lucy Park, NAVER Corp.
Masato Hagiwara, Duolingo Inc.
Dmitrijs Milajevs, NIST and Queen Mary University of London
Liling Tan, Rakuten Institute of Technology

Program Committee:

Martin Andrews, Red Cat Labs
Steven Bird, Charles Darwin University
Francis Bond, Nanyang Technological University
Jason Baldridge, Google
Steven Bethard, University of Arizona
Fred Blain, University of Sheffield
James Bradbury, Salesforce Research
Denny Britz, Prediction Machines
Marine Carpuat, University of Maryland
Kyunghyun Cho, New York University
Grzegorz Chrupała, Tilburg University
Hal Daumé III, University of Maryland
Jon Dehdari, Think Big Analytics
Christian Federmann, Microsoft Research
Mary Ellen Foster, University of Glasgow
Michael Wayne Goodman, University of Washington
Arwen Twinkle Griffioen, Zendesk Inc.
Joel Grus, Allen Institute for Artificial Intelligence
Chris Hokamp, Aylien Inc.
Matthew Honnibal, Explosion AI
Sung Kim, Hong Kong University of Science and Technology
Philipp Koehn, Johns Hopkins University
Taku Kudo, Google
Christopher Manning, Stanford University
Diana Maynard, University of Sheffield
Tomas Mikolov, Facebook AI Research (FAIR)
Ines Montani, Explosion AI
Andreas Müller, Columbia University
Graham Neubig, Carnegie Mellon University
Vlad Niculae, Cornell CIS
Joel Nothman, University of Sydney
Matt Post, Johns Hopkins University
David Przybilla, Idio
Amandalynne Paullada, University of Washington

Delip Rao, Joostware AI Research Corp
Radim Řehůřek, RaRe Technologies
Elijah Rippeth, MITRE Corporation
Abigail See, Stanford University
Carolina Scarton, University of Sheffield
Rico Sennrich, University of Edinburgh
Dan Simonson, Georgetown University
Vered Shwartz, Bar-Ilan University
Ian Soboroff, NIST
Pontus Stenetorp, University College London
Rachael Tatman, Kaggle
Tommaso Teofili, Adobe
Emiel van Miltenburg, Vrije Universiteit Amsterdam
Maarten van Gompel, Radboud University
Gaël Varoquaux, INRIA
KhengHui Yeo, Institute for Infocomm Research
Marcos Zampieri, University of Wolverhampton

Invited Speaker:

Joel Nothman, University of Sydney
Christopher Manning, Stanford University
Matthew Honnibal and Ines Montani, Explosion AI

Invited Talks

Open-Source Software's Responsibility to Science
Joel Nothman, University of Sydney

Stanford CoreNLP: 15 Years of Developing Academic Open Source Software
Christopher Manning, Stanford University

Reflections on Running spaCy: Commercial Open-source NLP
Matthew Honnibal and Ines Montani, Explosion AI

Open-Source Software's Responsibility to Science

Joel Nothman
University of Sydney

Abstract

Open-source software makes sophisticated technologies available to a wide audience. Arguably, most people applying language processing and machine learning techniques rely on popular open source tools targeted at these applications. Users may themselves be incapable of implementing the underlying algorithms. Users may or may not have extensive training to critically conduct experiments with these tools.

As maintainers of popular scientific software, we should be aware of our user base, and consider the ways in which our software design and documentation can lead or mislead users with respect to scientific best practices. In this talk, I will present some examples of these risks, primarily drawn from my experience developing Scikit-learn. For example: How can we help users avoid data leakage in cross-validation? How can we help users report precisely which algorithm or metric was used in an experiment?

Volunteer OSS maintainers have limited ability to see and manage these risks, and need the scientific community's assistance to get things right in design, implementation and documentation.

Biography

Joel Nothman began contributing to the Scientific Python ecosystem of open-source software as a research student at the University of Sydney in 2008. He has since made substantial contributions to the NLTK, Scipy, Pandas and IPython packages among others, but presently puts most of his open-source energies into maintaining Scikit-learn, a popular machine learning toolkit. Joel works as a data science research engineer at the University of Sydney, who fund some of his open-source development efforts. He completed his PhD on event reference there in 2014, and has been teaching their Natural Language Processing unit since 2016.

Stanford CoreNLP: 15 Years of Developing Academic Open Source Software

Christopher Manning
Stanford University

Abstract

My students and I at the Stanford NLP Group started releasing academic open source NLP software relatively early, in 2002. Over the years, the status and popularity of particular tools, and, since 2010, of the integrated Stanford CoreNLP offering has continually grown. It is not only used as a reliable tool — and easy mark to beat — in academic NLP, but it is widely used across government, non-profits, startups, and large companies. In this talk, I give my reflections on building academic open source software: what is required, what is important, and what is not so important; what we did right and what we did wrong; how a software project can be maintained long-term in such a context, how it adds to and detracts from doing academic research, narrowly defined; and how the world has changed and what the prospects are for the future.

Biography

Prof. Christopher Manning is the Thomas M. Siebel Professor in Machine Learning at Stanford University, in the Departments of Computer Science and Linguistics. He works on software that can intelligently process, understand, and generate human language material. He is a leader in applying Deep Learning to Natural Language Processing, with well-known research on the GloVe model of word vectors, Tree Recursive Neural Networks, sentiment analysis, neural network dependency parsing, neural machine translation, and deep language understanding. His computational linguistics work also covers probabilistic models of language, natural language inference and multilingual language processing, including being a principal developer of Stanford Dependencies and Universal Dependencies. Manning has coauthored leading textbooks on statistical approaches to Natural Language Processing (Manning and Schütze 1999) and information retrieval (Manning, Raghavan, and Schütze, 2008), as well as linguistic monographs on ergativity and complex predicates. Manning is an ACM Fellow, a AAAI Fellow, an ACL Fellow, and Past President of the ACL. Research of his has won ACL, Coling, EMNLP, and CHI Best Paper Awards. He has a B.A. (Hons) from The Australian National University, a Ph.D. from Stanford in 1994, and he held faculty positions at Carnegie Mellon University and the University of Sydney before returning to Stanford. He is a member of the Stanford NLP group and manages development of the Stanford CoreNLP software.

Reflections on Running spaCy: Commercial Open-source NLP

Matthew Honnibal and Ines Montani
Explosion AI

Abstract

In this talk, I'll share some lessons we've learned from running spaCy, the fastest-growing library for Natural Language Processing in Python, and provide our perspective on how to make commercial open-source work for both users and developers. Every open-source project must strike a balance between the responsibilities and control of the maintainers, and the responsibilities and control of the users. Understanding and communicating the motivations for publishing software under an open-source license can put less pressure on maintainers, and help users select projects appropriate for their requirements.

Biography

Ines Montani is the lead developer of Prodigy, and a core contributor to spaCy. Although a full-stack developer, Ines has particular expertise in front-end development, having started building websites when she was 11. Before founding Explosion AI, she was a freelance developer and strategist, using her four years executive experience in ad sales and digital marketing.

Matthew Honnibal began his research career as a linguist, completing his PhD in 2009 on lexicalised parsing with Combinatory Categorial Grammar, before working on incremental speech parsing. These days he is best known as a software engineer, for his work on the spaCy NLP library. He grew up in Sydney, lives in Berlin, and still misses CCG.

Table of Contents

Conference Program

Friday, July 20, 2018

8:45–9:00 ***Loading Presentations to Computer***

9:00–9:05 ***Opening Remarks***

9:05–9:50 ***Invited Talk 1 (Joel Nothman)***

9:50–10:30 ***Lightning Presentation for Posters Session 1***

10:30–11:00 ***Coffee Break***

11:00–11:45 ***Poster Session 1***

AllenNLP: A Deep Semantic Natural Language Processing Platform
Matt Gardner, Joel Grus, Mark Neumann, Oyvind Tafjord, Pradeep Dasigi, Nelson F. Liu, Matthew Peters, Michael Schmitz and Luke Zettlemoyer

Stop Word Lists in Free Open-source Software Packages
Joel Nothman, Hanmin Qin and Roman Yurchak

Texar: A Modularized, Versatile, and Extensible Toolbox for Text Generation
Zhiting Hu, Zichao Yang, Tiancheng Zhao, Haoran Shi, Junxian He, Di Wang, Xuezhe Ma, Zhengzhong Liu, Xiaodan Liang, Lianhui Qin, Devendra Singh Chaplot, Bowen Tan, Xingjiang Yu and Eric Xing

The ACL Anthology: Current State and Future Directions
Daniel Gildea, Min-Yen Kan, Nitin Madnani, Christoph Teichmann and Martin Villalba

The risk of sub-optimal use of Open Source NLP Software: UKB is inadvertently state-of-the-art in knowledge-based WSD
Eneko Agirre, Oier Lopez de Lacalle and Aitor Soroa

12:00–14:00 ***Lunch***

Friday, July 20, 2018 (continued)

14:00–14:45 ***Invited Talk 2 (Christopher Manning)***

14:45–15:30 ***Lightning Presentation for Posters 2***

15:30–16:00 ***Break***

16:00–16:45 ***Poster Session 2***

Baseline: A Library for Rapid Modeling, Experimentation and Development of Deep Learning Algorithms targeting NLP
Daniel Pressel, Sagnik Ray Choudhury, Brian Lester, Yanjie Zhao and Matt Barta

OpenSeq2Seq: Extensible Toolkit for Distributed and Mixed Precision Training of Sequence-to-Sequence Models
Oleksii Kuchaiev, Boris Ginsburg, Igor Gitman, Vitaly Lavrukhin, Carl Case and Paulius Micikevicius

Integrating Multiple NLP Technologies into an Open-source Platform for Multilingual Media Monitoring
Ulrich Germann, Renars Liepins, Didzis Gosko and Guntis Barzdins

The Annotated Transformer
Alexander Rush

16:45–17:30 ***Invited Talk 3 (Matthew Honnibal and Ines Montani)***

17:30–1735 ***Closing Remarks***

AllenNLP: A Deep Semantic Natural Language Processing Platform

**Matt Gardner, Joel Grus, Mark Neumann, Oyvind Tafjord, Pradeep Dasigi,
Nelson F. Liu, Matthew Peters, Michael Schmitz, Luke Zettlemoyer**
Allen Institute for Artificial Intelligence

Abstract

Modern natural language processing (NLP) research requires writing code. Ideally this code would provide a precise definition of the approach, easy repeatability of results, and a basis for extending the research. However, many research codebases bury high-level parameters under implementation details, are challenging to run and debug, and are difficult enough to extend that they are more likely to be rewritten. This paper describes AllenNLP, a library for applying deep learning methods to NLP research, which addresses these issues with easy-to-use command-line tools, declarative configuration-driven experiments, and modular NLP abstractions. AllenNLP has already increased the rate of research experimentation and the sharing of NLP components at the Allen Institute for Artificial Intelligence, and we are working to have the same impact across the field.

1 Introduction

Neural network models are now the state-of-the-art for a wide range of tasks such as text classification (Howard and Ruder, 2018), machine translation (Vaswani et al., 2017), semantic role labeling (Zhou and Xu, 2015; He et al., 2017), coreference resolution (Lee et al., 2017a), and semantic parsing (Krishnamurthy et al., 2017). However it can be surprisingly difficult to tune new models or replicate existing results. State-of-the-art deep learning models often take over a week to train on modern GPUs and are sensitive to initialization and hyperparameter settings. Furthermore, reference implementations often re-implement NLP components from scratch and make it difficult to reproduce results, creating a barrier to entry for research on many problems.

AllenNLP, a platform for research on deep learning methods in natural language processing, is designed to address these problems and to significantly lower barriers to high quality NLP research by

- implementing useful NLP abstractions that make it easy to write higher-level model code for a broad range of NLP tasks, swap out components, and re-use implementations,
- handling common NLP deep learning problems, such as masking and padding, and keeping these low-level details separate from the high-level model and experiment definitions,
- defining experiments using declarative configuration files, which provide a high-level summary of a model and its training, and make it easy to change the deep learning architecture and tune hyper-parameters, and
- sharing models through live demos, making complex NLP accessible and debug-able.

The AllenNLP website[1] provides tutorials, API documentation, pretrained models, and source code[2]. The AllenNLP platform has a permissive Apache 2.0 license and is easy to download and install via pip, a Docker image, or cloning the GitHub repository. It includes reference implementations for recent state-of-the-art models (see Section 3) that can be easily run (to make predictions on arbitrary new inputs) and retrained with different parameters or on new data. These pretrained models have interactive online demos[3]

[1]http://allennlp.org/
[2]http://github.com/allenai/allennlp
[3]http://demo.allennlp.org/

Proceedings of Workshop for NLP Open Source Software, pages 1–6

with visualizations to help interpret model decisions and make predictions accessible to others. The reference implementations provide examples of the framework functionality (Section 2) and also serve as baselines for future research.

AllenNLP is an ongoing open-source effort maintained by several full-time engineers and researchers at the Allen Institute for Artificial Intelligence, as well as interns from top PhD programs and contributors from the broader NLP community. It is used widespread internally for research on common sense, logical reasoning, and state-of-the-art NLP components such as: constituency parsers, semantic parsing, and word representations. AllenNLP is gaining traction externally and we want to invest to make it the standard for advancing NLP research using PyTorch.

2 Library Design

AllenNLP is a platform designed specifically for deep learning and NLP research. AllenNLP is built on PyTorch (Paszke et al., 2017), which provides many attractive features for NLP research. PyTorch supports dynamic networks, has a clean "Pythonic" syntax, and is easy to use.

The AllenNLP library provides (1) a flexible data API that handles intelligent batching and padding, (2) high-level abstractions for common operations in working with text, and (3) a modular and extensible experiment framework that makes doing good science easy.

AllenNLP maintains a high test coverage of over 90%[4] to ensure its components and models are working as intended. Library features are built with testability in mind so new components can maintain a similar test coverage.

2.1 Text Data Processing

AllenNLP's data processing API is built around the notion of `Fields`. Each `Field` represents a single input array to a model. `Fields` are grouped together in `Instances` that represent the examples for training or prediction.

The `Field` API is flexible and easy to extend, allowing for a unified data API for tasks as diverse as tagging, semantic role labeling, question answering, and textual entailment. To represent the SQuAD dataset (Rajpurkar et al., 2016), for example, which has a question and a passage as inputs and a span from the passage as output, each training `Instance` comprises a `TextField` for the question, a `TextField` for the passage, and a `SpanField` representing the start and end positions of the answer in the passage.

The user need only read data into a set of `Instance` objects with the desired fields, and the library can automatically sort them into batches with similar sequence lengths, pad all sequences in each batch to the same length, and randomly shuffle the batches for input to a model.

2.2 NLP-Focused Abstractions

AllenNLP provides a high-level API for building models, with abstractions designed specifically for NLP research. By design, the code for a model actually specifies a *class* of related models. The researcher can then experiment with various architectures within this class by simply changing a configuration file, without having to change any code.

The library has many abstractions that encapsulate common decision points in NLP models. Key examples are: (1) how text is represented as vectors, (2) how vector sequences are modified to produce new vector sequences, (3) how vector sequences are merged into a single vector.

`TokenEmbedder`: This abstraction takes input arrays generated by e.g. a `TextField` and returns a sequence of vector embeddings. Through the use of polymorphism and AllenNLP's experiment framework (see Section 2.3), researchers can easily switch between a wide variety of possible word representations. Simply by changing a configuration file, an experimenter can choose between pre-trained word embeddings, word embeddings concatenated with a character-level CNN encoding, or even pre-trained model token-in-context embeddings (Peters et al., 2017), which allows for easy controlled experimentation.

`Seq2SeqEncoder`: A common operation in deep NLP models is to take a sequence of word vectors and pass them through a recurrent network to encode contextual information, producing a new sequence of vectors as output. There is a large number of ways to do this, including LSTMs (Hochreiter and Schmidhuber, 1997), GRUs (Cho et al., 2014), intra-sentence attention (Cheng et al., 2016), recurrent additive networks (Lee et al., 2017b), and many more. AllenNLP's `Seq2SeqEncoder` abstracts away the decision of which particular encoder to use, allow-

[4] https://codecov.io/gh/allenai/allennlp

ing the user to build an encoder-agnostic model and specify the encoder via configuration. In this way, a researcher can easily explore new recurrent architectures; for example, they can replace the LSTMs in *any model* that uses this abstraction with any other encoder, measuring the impact across a wide range of models and tasks.

Seq2VecEncoder: Another common operation in NLP models is to merge a sequence of vectors into a single vector, using either a recurrent network with some kind of averaging or pooling, or using a convolutional network. This operation is encapsulated in AllenNLP by a `Seq2VecEncoder`. This abstraction again allows the model code to only describe a *class* of similar models, with particular instantiations of that model class being determined by a configuration file.

SpanExtractor: A recent trend in NLP is to build models that operate on *spans* of text, instead of on *tokens*. State-of-the-art models for coreference resolution (Lee et al., 2017a), constituency parsing (Stern et al., 2017), and semantic role labeling (He et al., 2017) all operate in this way. Support for building this kind of model is built into AllenNLP, including a `SpanExtractor` abstraction that determines how span vectors get computed from sequences of token vectors.

2.3 Experimental Framework

The primary design goal of AllenNLP is to make it easy to do good science with controlled experiments. Because of the abstractions described in Section 2.2, large parts of the model architecture and training-related hyper-parameters can be configured outside of model code. This makes it easy to clearly specify the important decisions that define a new model in configuration, and frees the researcher from needing to code all of the implementation details from scratch.

This architecture design is accomplished in AllenNLP using a HOCON[5] configuration file that specifies, e.g., which text representations and encoders to use in an experiment. The mapping from strings in the configuration file to instantiated objects in code is done through the use of a *registry*, which allows users of the library to add new implementations of any of the provided abstractions, or even to create their own new abstractions.

While some entries in the configuration file are optional, many are required and if unspecified AllenNLP will raise a ConfigurationError when reading the configuration. Additionally, when a configuration file is loaded, AllenNLP logs the configuration values, providing a record of both specified and default parameters for your model.

3 Reference Models

AllenNLP includes reference implementations of widely used language understanding models. These models demonstrate how to use the framework functionality presented in Section 2. They also have verified performance levels that closely match the original results, and can serve as comparison baselines for future research.

AllenNLP includes reference implementations for several tasks, including:

- **Semantic Role Labeling** (SRL) models recover the latent predicate argument structure of a sentence (Palmer et al., 2005). SRL builds representations that answer basic questions about sentence meaning; for example, "who" did "what" to "whom." The AllenNLP SRL model is a re-implementation of a deep BiLSTM model (He et al., 2017). The implemented model closely matches the published model which was state of the art in 2017, achieving a F1 of 78.9% on English Ontonotes 5.0 dataset using the CoNLL 2011/12 shared task format.

- **Machine Comprehension** (MC) systems take an evidence text and a question as input, and predict a span within the evidence that answers the question. AllenNLP includes a reference implementation of the BiDAF MC model (Seo et al., 2017) which was state of the art for the SQuAD benchmark (Rajpurkar et al., 2016) in early 2017.

- **Textual Entailment** (TE) models take a pair of sentences and predict whether the facts in the first necessarily imply the facts in the second. The AllenNLP TE model is a re-implementation of the decomposable attention model (Parikh et al., 2016), a widely used TE baseline that was state-of-the-art on the SNLI dataset (Bowman et al., 2015) in late 2016. The AllenNLP TE model achieves

[5]We use it as JSON with comments. See https://github.com/lightbend/config/blob/master/HOCON.md for the full spec.

an accuracy of 86.4% on the SNLI 1.0 test dataset, a 2% improvement on most publicly available implementations and a similar score as the original paper. Rather than pre-trained Glove vectors, this model uses ELMo embeddings (Peters et al., 2018), which are completely character based and account for the 2% improvement.

- A **Constituency Parser** breaks a text into sub-phrases, or constituents. Non-terminals in the tree are types of phrases and the terminals are the words in the sentence. The AllenNLP constituency parser is an implementation of a minimal neural model for constituency parsing based on an independent scoring of labels and spans (Stern et al., 2017). This model uses ELMo embeddings (Peters et al., 2018), which are completely character based and improves single model performance from 92.6 F1 to 94.11 F1 on the Penn Tree bank, a 20% relative error reduction.

AllenNLP also includes a token embedder that uses pre-trained ELMo (Peters et al., 2018) representations. ELMo is a deep contextualized word representation that models both complex characteristics of word use (e.g., syntax and semantics) and how these uses vary across linguistic contexts (in order to model polysemy). ELMo embeddings significantly improve the state of the art across a broad range of challenging NLP problems, including question answering, textual entailment, and sentiment analysis.

Additional models are currently under development and are regularly released, including semantic parsing (Krishnamurthy et al., 2017) and multi-paragraph reading comprehension (Clark and Gardner, 2017). We expect the number of tasks and reference implementations to grow steadily over time. The most up-to-date list of reference models is maintained at http://allennlp.org/models.

4 Related Work

Many existing NLP pipelines, such as Stanford CoreNLP (Manning et al., 2014) and spaCy[6], focus on predicting linguistic structures rather than modeling NLP architectures. While AllenNLP supports making predictions using pre-trained models, its core focus is on enabling novel research. This emphasis on configuring parameters, training, and evaluating is similar to Weka (Witten and Frank, 1999) or Scikit-learn (Pedregosa et al., 2011), but AllenNLP focuses on cutting-edge research in deep learning and is designed around declarative configuration of model architectures in addition to model parameters.

Most existing deep-learning toolkits are designed for general machine learning (Bergstra et al., 2010; Yu et al., 2014; Chen et al., 2015; Abadi et al., 2016; Neubig et al., 2017), and can require significant effort to develop research infrastructure for particular model classes. Some, such as Keras (Chollet et al., 2015), do aim to make it easy to build deep learning models. Similar to how AllenNLP is an abstraction layer on top of PyTorch, Keras provides high-level abstractions on top of static graph frameworks such as TensorFlow. While Keras' abstractions and functionality are useful for general machine learning, they are somewhat lacking for NLP, where input data types can be very complex and dynamic graph frameworks are more often necessary.

Finally, AllenNLP is related to toolkits for deep learning research in dialog (Miller et al., 2017) and machine translation (Klein et al., 2017). Those toolkits support learning general functions that map strings (e.g. foreign language text or user utterances) to strings (e.g. English text or system responses). AllenNLP, in contrast, is a more general library for building models for any kind of NLP task, including text classification, constituency parsing, textual entailment, question answering, and more.

5 Conclusion

The design of AllenNLP allows researchers to focus on the high-level summary of their models rather than the details, and to do careful, reproducible research. Internally at the Allen Institute for Artificial Intelligence the library is widely adopted and has improved the quality of our research code, spread knowledge about deep learning, and made it easier to share discoveries between teams. AllenNLP is gaining traction externally and is growing an open-source community of contributors [7]. The AllenNLP team is com-

[6]https://spacy.io/

[7]See GitHub stars and issues on https://github.com/allenai/allennlp and mentions from publications at https://www.semanticscholar.org/search?q=allennlp.

mitted to continuing work on this library in order to enable better research practices throughout the NLP community and to build a community of researchers who maintain a collection of the best models in natural language processing.

References

Martín Abadi, Ashish Agarwal, Paul Barham, Eugene Brevdo, Zhifeng Chen, Craig Citro, Greg S Corrado, Andy Davis, Jeffrey Dean, Matthieu Devin, et al. 2016. Tensorflow: Large-scale machine learning on heterogeneous distributed systems. *CoRR abs/1603.04467*.

James Bergstra, Olivier Breuleux, Frédéric Bastien, Pascal Lamblin, Razvan Pascanu, Guillaume Desjardins, Joseph Turian, David Warde-Farley, and Yoshua Bengio. 2010. Theano: A cpu and gpu math compiler in python. In *Proc. 9th Python in Science Conf*, pages 1–7.

Samuel R. Bowman, Gabor Angeli, Christopher Potts, and Christopher D. Manning. 2015. A large annotated corpus for learning natural language inference. In *Proceedings of the Conference on Empirical Methods in Natural Language Processing (EMNLP)*. Association for Computational Linguistics.

Tianqi Chen, Mu Li, Yutian Li, Min Lin, Naiyan Wang, Minjie Wang, Tianjun Xiao, Bing Xu, Chiyuan Zhang, and Zheng Zhang. 2015. Mxnet: A flexible and efficient machine learning library for heterogeneous distributed systems. *CoRR abs/1512.01274*.

Jianpeng Cheng, Li Dong, and Mirella Lapata. 2016. Long short-term memory-networks for machine reading. In *Proceedings of the Conference on Empirical Methods in Natural Language Processing (EMNLP)*.

Kyunghyun Cho, Bart van Merrienboer, Çaglar Gülçehre, Dzmitry Bahdanau, Fethi Bougares, Holger Schwenk, and Yoshua Bengio. 2014. Learning phrase representations using RNN encoder-decoder for statistical machine translation. In *Proceedings of the Conference on Empirical Methods in Natural Language Processing, (EMNLP)*, pages 1724–1734.

François Chollet et al. 2015. Keras. `https://keras.io`.

Christopher T Clark and Matthew Gardner. 2017. Simple and effective multi-paragraph reading comprehension. *CoRR*, abs/1710.10723.

Luheng He, Kenton Lee, Mike Lewis, and Luke Zettlemoyer. 2017. Deep semantic role labeling: What works and whats next. In *Proceedings of the Association for Computational Linguistics (ACL)*.

Sepp Hochreiter and Jürgen Schmidhuber. 1997. Long short-term memory. *Neural computation*, 9(8):1735–1780.

Jeremy Howard and Sebastian Ruder. 2018. Fine-tuned language models for text classification. *CoRR*, abs/1801.06146.

Guillaume Klein, Yoon Kim, Yuntian Deng, Jean Senellart, and Alexander M. Rush. 2017. Opennmt: Open-source toolkit for neural machine translation. In *Proceedings of the 55th Annual Meeting of the Association for Computational Linguistics, ACL*, pages 67–72.

Jayant Krishnamurthy, Pradeep Dasigi, and Matthew Gardner. 2017. Neural semantic parsing with type constraints for semi-structured tables. In *EMNLP*.

Kenton Lee, Luheng He, Mike Lewis, and Luke Zettlemoyer. 2017a. End-to-end neural coreference resolution. In *Proceedings of the Conference on Empirical Methods in Natural Language Processing (EMNLP)*.

Kenton Lee, Omer Levy, and Luke Zettlemoyer. 2017b. Recurrent additive networks. *CoRR abs/1705.07393*.

Christopher D Manning, Mihai Surdeanu, John Bauer, Jenny Rose Finkel, Steven Bethard, and David McClosky. 2014. The stanford corenlp natural language processing toolkit. In *Proceedings of the Association for Computational Linguistics (ACL) (System Demonstrations)*.

Alexander H. Miller, Will Feng, Dhruv Batra, Antoine Bordes, Adam Fisch, Jiasen Lu, Devi Parikh, and Jason Weston. 2017. Parlai: A dialog research software platform. In *Proceedings of the Conference on Empirical Methods in Natural Language Processing, EMNLP*, pages 79–84.

Graham Neubig, Chris Dyer, Yoav Goldberg, Austin Matthews, Waleed Ammar, Antonios Anastasopoulos, Miguel Ballesteros, David Chiang, Daniel Clothiaux, Trevor Cohn, et al. 2017. Dynet: The dynamic neural network toolkit. *CoRR abs/1701.03980*.

Martha Palmer, Daniel Gildea, and Paul Kingsbury. 2005. The proposition bank: An annotated corpus of semantic roles. *Computational linguistics*, 31(1):71–106.

Ankur P Parikh, Oscar Täckström, Dipanjan Das, and Jakob Uszkoreit. 2016. A decomposable attention model for natural language inference. In *Proceedings of the Conference on Empirical Methods in Natural Language Processing (EMNLP)*.

Adam Paszke, Sam Gross, Soumith Chintala, Gregory Chanan, Edward Yang, Zachary DeVito, Zeming Lin, Alban Desmaison, Luca Antiga, and Adam Lerer. 2017. Automatic differentiation in pytorch. In *NIPS-W*.

F. Pedregosa, G. Varoquaux, A. Gramfort, V. Michel, B. Thirion, O. Grisel, M. Blondel, P. Prettenhofer, R. Weiss, V. Dubourg, J. Vanderplas, A. Passos, D. Cournapeau, M. Brucher, M. Perrot, and E. Duchesnay. 2011. Scikit-learn: Machine learning in Python. *Journal of Machine Learning Research*, 12:2825–2830.

Matthew E Peters, Waleed Ammar, Chandra Bhagavatula, and Russell Power. 2017. Semi-supervised sequence tagging with bidirectional language models. In *Proceedings of the Association for Computational Linguistics (ACL)*.

Matthew E. Peters, Mark Neumann, Mohit Iyyer, Matthew Gardner, Christopher T Clark, Kenton Lee, and Luke S. Zettlemoyer. 2018. Deep contextualized word representations. *CoRR*, abs/1802.05365.

Pranav Rajpurkar, Jian Zhang, Konstantin Lopyrev, and Percy Liang. 2016. Squad: 100,000+ questions for machine comprehension of text. In *Proceedings of the Conference on Empirical Methods in Natural Language Processing (EMNLP)*.

Minjoon Seo, Aniruddha Kembhavi, Ali Farhadi, and Hannaneh Hajishirzi. 2017. Bidirectional attention flow for machine comprehension.

Mitchell Stern, Jacob Andreas, and Dan Klein. 2017. A minimal span-based neural constituency parser. In *ACL*.

Ashish Vaswani, Noam Shazeer, Niki Parmar, Jakob Uszkoreit, Llion Jones, Aidan N. Gomez, Lukasz Kaiser, and Illia Polosukhin. 2017. Attention is all you need. In *NIPS*.

Ian H. Witten and Eibe Frank. 1999. Data mining: Practical machine learning tools and techniques with java implementations.

Dong Yu, Adam Eversole, Mike Seltzer, Kaisheng Yao, Zhiheng Huang, Brian Guenter, Oleksii Kuchaiev, Yu Zhang, Frank Seide, Huaming Wang, et al. 2014. An introduction to computational networks and the computational network toolkit. *Microsoft Technical Report MSR-TR-2014–112*.

Jie Zhou and Wei Xu. 2015. End-to-end learning of semantic role labeling using recurrent neural networks. In *Proceedings of the Association for Computational Linguistics (ACL)*.

Stop Word Lists in Free Open-source Software Packages

Joel Nothman
Sydney Informatics Hub
University of Sydney
joel.nothman@gmail.com

Hanmin Qin
Peking University
qinhanmin2005@sina.com

Roman Yurchak
Symerio
rth.yurchak@gmail.com

Abstract

Open-source software (OSS) packages for natural language processing often include stop word lists. Users may apply them without awareness of their surprising omissions (e.g. *hasn't* but not *hadn't*) and inclusions (e.g. *computer*), or their incompatibility with particular tokenizers. Motivated by issues raised about the Scikit-learn stop list, we investigate variation among and consistency within 52 popular English-language stop lists, and propose strategies for mitigating these issues.

1 Introduction

Open-source software (OSS) resources tend to become de-facto standards by virtue of their availability and popular use. Resources include tokenization rules and stop word lists, whose precise definitions are essential for reproducible and interpretable models. These resources can be selected somewhat arbitrarily by OSS contributors, such that their popularity within the community may not be a reflection of their quality, universality or suitability for a particular task. Users may then be surprised by behaviors such as the word *computer* being eliminated from their text analysis due to its inclusion in a popular stop list.

This paper brings to the community's attention some issues recently identified in the Scikit-learn stop list. Despite is popular use, the current Scikit-learn maintainers cannot justify the use of this particular list, and are unaware of how it was constructed. This spurs us to investigate variation among and consistency within popular English-language stop lists provided in several popular language processing, retrieval and machine learning libraries. We then make recommendations for improving stop list provision in OSS.

2 Background

Stop words are presumed to be not informative as to the meaning of documents, and hence are defined by being unusually frequent, or by not being "content words". Saif et al. (2014) lists several methods for constructing a stop word list, including: manual construction; words with high *document frequency* or total *term frequency* in a corpus; or by comparing term frequency statistics from a sample of documents with those in a larger collection.[1] In practice, Manning et al. (2008) indicate that statistical approaches tend not to be used alone, but are combined with manual filtering. This paper notes ways in which statistical construction of stop lists may have introduced regrettable errors.

Stop lists have been generated for other languages, such as Chinese (Zou et al., 2006), Thai (Daowadung and Chen, 2012) and Farsi (Sadeghi and Vegas, 2014), using uses similar frequency threshold approaches, are susceptible to the same issues discussed here.

Most prior work focuses on assessing or improving the effectiveness of stop word lists, such as Schofield et al.'s (2017) recent critique of stop lists in topic modeling. Our work instead examines what is available and widely used.

3 Case Study: Scikit-learn

Having become aware of issues with the Scikit-learn (Pedregosa et al., 2011) stop list,[2] we begin by studying it. Scikit-learn provides out-of-the-box feature extraction tools which convert a collection of text documents to a matrix of token counts, optionally removing n-grams containing

[1] They also investigate using supervised feature selection techniques, but the supervised learning context is inapplicable here.

[2] As at version 0.19.1

Proceedings of Workshop for NLP Open Source Software, pages 7–12
Melbourne, Australia, July 20, 2018.

given stop words. Being a popular library for machine learning, many of its users take a naive approach to language processing, and are unlikely to take a nuanced approach to stop word removal.

History While users are able to provide their own stop list, Scikit-learn provides an English-language list since July 2010. The list was initially disabled by default since the contributing author claimed that it did not improve accuracy for text classification (see commit `41b0562`). In November 2010, another contributor argued to enable the list by default, saying that stop word removal is a reasonable default behavior (commit `41128af`). The developers disabled the list by default again in March 2012 (commit `a510d17`).

The list was copied from the Glasgow Information Retrieval Group,[3] but it was unattributed until January 2012 (commit `d4c4c6f`). The list was altered in 2011 to remove the content word *computer* (commit `cdf7df9`), and in 2015 to correct the word *fify* to *fifty* (commit `3e4ebac`).

This history gives a sense of how a stop word list may be selected and provided without great awareness of its content: its provenance was initially disregarded; and some words were eventually deemed inappropriate.

Critique Currently, the list in Scikit-learn has several issues. Firstly, the list is incompatible with the tokenizer provided along with it. It includes words discarded by the default tokenizer, i.e., words less than 2 chars (e.g. *i*), and some abbreviated forms which will be split by the tokenizer (e.g. *hasnt*). What's more, it excludes enclitics generated by the tokenizer (e.g. *ve* of *we've*). In April 2017, a maintainer proposed to add *ve* to the list.[4] Contributors argued this would break reproducibility across software versions, and the issue remains unresolved.

Secondly, there are some controversial words in the list, such as *system* and *cry*. These words are considered to be informative and are seldom included in other stop lists. In March 2018, a user requested the removal of *system* and has gained approval from the community.[5]

Another issue is that the list has some surprising omissions. Compared to extensions of the Glasgow IR list from Stone et al. (2010) used by spaCy (Honnibal and Montani, 2017) and gensim (Řehůřek and Sojka, 2010), the list in Scikit-learn includes modal *has*, but lacks *does*; includes intensifier *very* but excludes *really*; and includes light verb *get* but excludes *make*.

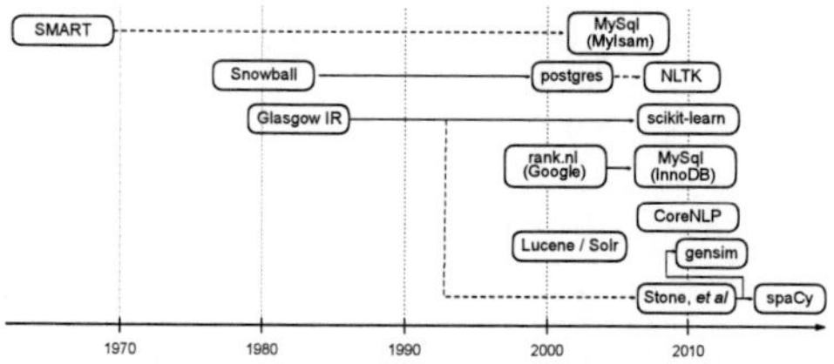

Figure 1: Family tree of popular stop word lists.

The Glasgow IR list appears to have been constructed from corpus statistics, although typographic errors like *fify* suggest manual editing. However, we have not found any documentation about how the Glasgow IR list was constructed. Hence we know little about how to generate comparable lists for other languages or domains.

In the remainder of this paper, we consider how similar issues apply to other open-source stop lists.

4 Datasets

We conduct our experiments on Igor Brigadir's collection of English-language stop word lists.[6] We exclude 1 empty list, 2 lists which contain n-grams ($n > 1$) and 1 list which is intended to augment other lists (i.e. LEMUR's forumstop). Finally, we get 52 lists extracted from various search engines, libraries, and articles. The size of the lists varies (see the right part of Figure 2), from 24 words in the EBSCOhost medical databases list, to 988 words in the ATIRE search engine list.

5 Stop List Families

Through digging into project history, we construct a family tree of some popular stop lists (Figure 1) to show how popular OSS packages adopt or adapt existing lists. Solid lines in the figure correspond to inclusion without major modification, while dashed lines correspond to a more loose adaptation. For instance, the Glasgow IR list used by Scikit-learn was extended with 18 more words by

[3] `http://ir.dcs.gla.ac.uk/resources/linguistic_utils/stop_words`

[4] `https://github.com/scikit-learn/scikit-learn/issues/8687`

[5] `https://github.com/scikit-learn/scikit-learn/issues/10735`

[6] `https://github.com/igorbrigadir/stopwords/tree/21fb2ef`

Stone et al. (2010), and this list was adopted by OSS packages gensim and spaCy in turn.

A more data driven approach identifies similarities among stop lists by clustering them with the Jaccard distance metric ($JD(A, B) := 1 - \frac{|A \cap B|}{|A \cup B|}$ where A and B are sets of stop words). In Figure 2, we have plotted the same data with a heatmap of word inclusion in order of descending document frequency in the NYT section of Gigaword 5.0 (Parker et al., 2011). Here we take the maximum frequency under three tokenizers from Lucene, Scikit-learn and spaCy. Each of them has different approaches to enclitics (e.g. *hasn't* is treated as *hasn't* in Lucene; *hasn* in Scikit-learn and *has n't* in spaCy).

Looking at the heatmap, we see that stop words are largely concentrated around high document frequency. Some high frequency words are absent from many stop lists because most stop lists assume particular tokenization strategies (See Section 6.2). However, beyond the extremely frequent words, even the shortest lists vary widely in which words they then include. Some stop lists include many relatively low-frequency words. This is most noticeable for large lists like TERRIER and ATIRE-Puurula. TERRIER goes to pains to include synthesized inflectional variants, even *concerninger*, and archaic forms, like *couldst*.

Through the clusermap, we find some lists with very high within-cluster similarity ($JD < 0.2$): Ranks.nl old Google list and MySQL/InnoDB list; PostgreSQL list and NLTK list; Weka list, MALLET list, MySQL-MyISAM list, SMART list and ROUGE list; Glasgow IR list, Scikit-learn list and spaCy/Gensim list. Beyond these simple clusters, some lists appear to have surprisingly high overlap (usually asymmetric): Stanford CoreNLP list appears to be an extension of Snowball's original list; ATIRE-Puurula appears to be an extension of the Ranks.nl Large list.

6 Common Issues for Stop Word Lists

In section 3, we find several issues in the stop word list from Scikit-learn. In this section, we explore how these problems manifest in other lists.

6.1 Controversial Words

We consider words which appear in less than 10% of lists to be controversial.[7] After excluding words which do not begin with English characters, we get 2066 distinct stop words in the 52 lists. Among these words, 1396 (67.6%) words only appear in less than 10% of lists, and 807 (39.1%) words only appear in 1 list (see the bars at the top of Figure 2), indicating that controversial words cover a large proportion. On the contrary, only 64 (3.1%) words are accepted by more than 80% lists. Among the 52 lists, 45 have controversial words.

We further investigate the document frequency of these controversial words using Google Books Ngrams (Michel et al., 2011). Figure 3 shows the document frequency distribution. Note: We scale document frequency of controversial words by the max document frequency among all the words. Although peaked on rare words, some words are frequent (e.g. *general, great, time*), indicating that the problem is not trivial.

6.2 Tokenization and Stop Lists

Popular software libraries apply different tokenization rules, particularly with respect to word-internal punctuation. By comparing how different stop lists handle the word *doesn't* in Figure 4, we see several approaches: most lists stop *doesn't*. A few stop *doesn* or *doesnt*, but none stop both of these. Two stop *doesn't* as well as *doesnt*, which may help them be robust to different choices of tokenizer, or may be designed to handle informal text where apostrophes may be elided.

However, we find tools providing lists that are inconsistent with their tokenizers. While most lists stop *not*, Penn Treebank-style tokenizers – provided by CoreNLP, spaCy, NLTK and other NLP-oriented packages – also generate the token *n't*. Of our dataset, *n't* is only stopped by CoreNLP.[8] Weka and Scikit-learn both have default tokenizers which delimit tokens at punctuation including ', yet neither stops words like *doesn*.

We find similar results when repeating this analysis on other negated models (e.g. *hasn't, haven't, wouldn't*), showing that stop lists are often tuned to particular tokenizers, albeit not always the default tokenizer provided by the corresponding package. More generally, we have not found any OSS package which documents how tokenization relates to the choice of stop list.

[7]Some false negatives will result from the shared origins of lists detailed in the previous section, but we find very similar results if we remove near-duplicate lists (Jaccard distance < 0.2) from our experiments.

[8]We are aware that spaCy, in commit `f708d74`, recently amended its list to improve consistency with its tokenizer, adding *n't* among other Penn Treebank contraction tokens.

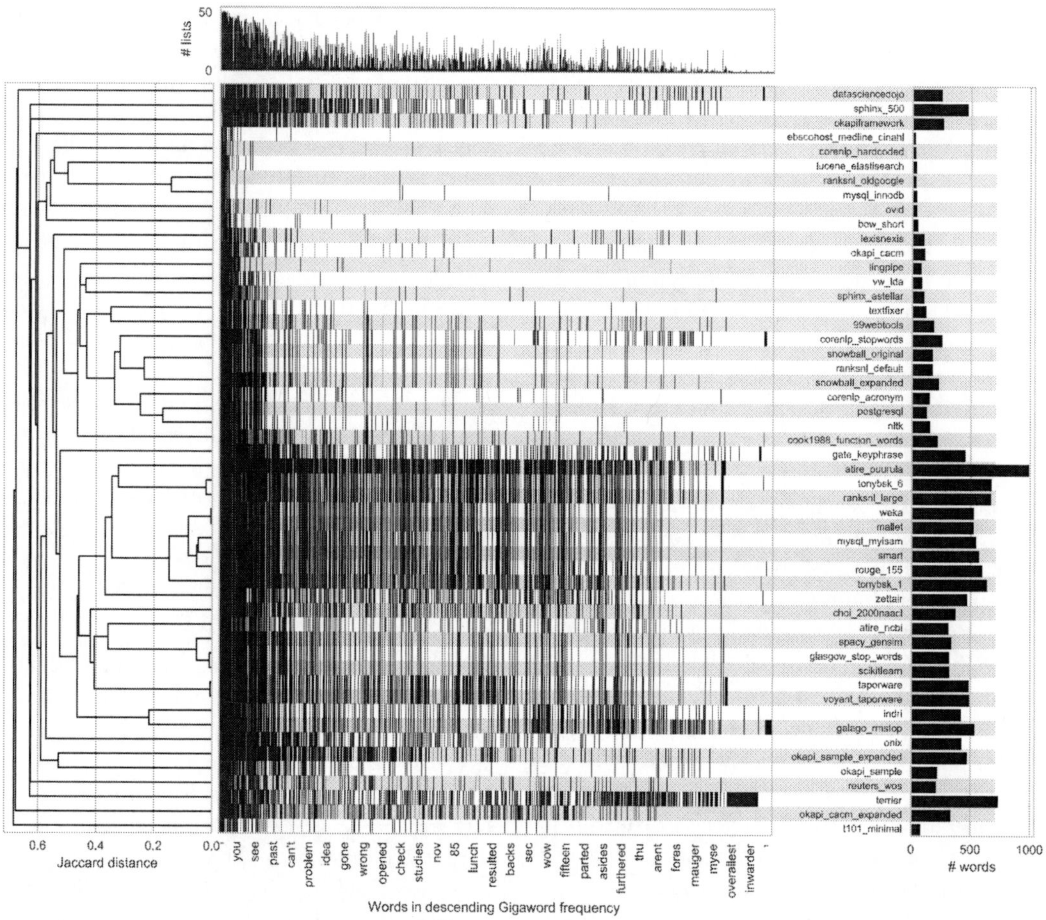

Figure 2: Word inclusion in clustered English stop word lists. Words are ordered by descending document frequency. The dendrogram on the left indicates minimum Jaccard distance between stop list pairs when merged. The bars on the right show the number of words in each list, and the bars on the top indicate the number of lists each word is found in.

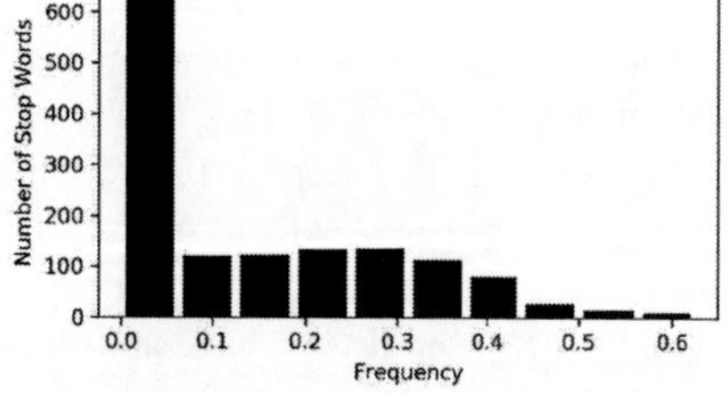

Figure 3: Document frequency distribution of controversial words

6.3 Incompleteness

Stop lists generated exclusively from corpus statistics are bound to omit some inflectional forms of an included word, as well as related lexemes, such as less frequent members of a functional syntactic class. In particular, stop word list construction prefers frequency criteria over contextual indicators of a word's function, despite Harris's (1954) well-established theory that similar words (e.g. function words, light verbs, negated modals) should appear in similar contexts.

To continue the example of negated modals, we find inconsistencies in the inclusion of *have* and its variants, summarized in Figure 5. Weka includes *has*, but omits its negated forms, despite including *not*. Conversely, Okapi includes *doesnt*, but omits

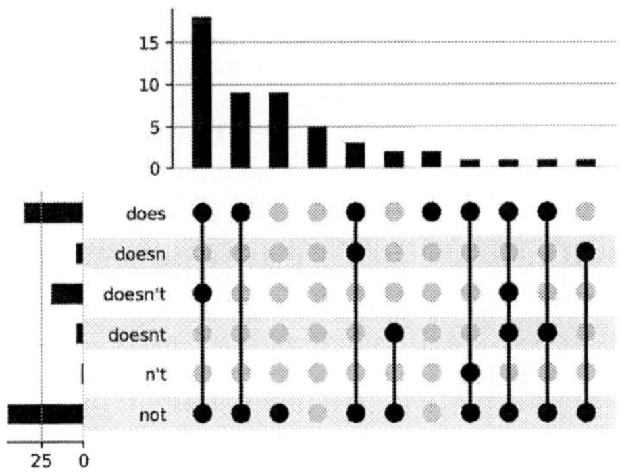

Figure 4: Number of stop lists that include variants of *doesn't* and their combinations.

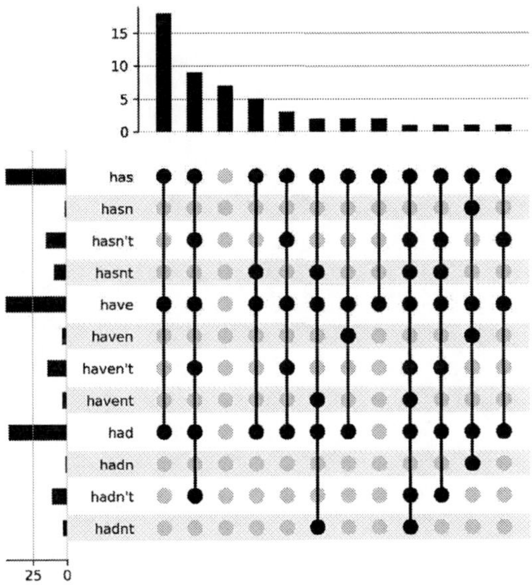

Figure 5: Number of stop lists that include variants of *have* and their combinations.

does. Several lists include *has*, *hasnt*, *have* and *had*, but omits *havent* and *hadnt*. Several lists that include *has* and *have* forms omit *had* forms. These inclusions and omissions seem arbitrary.

Some negated modals like *shan't* and *mustn't* are absent more often than other modals (e.g. *doesn't*, *hasn't*), which may be an unsurprising artifact of their frequency, or may be an ostensive omission because they are more marked.

TERRIER list (Ounis et al., 2005) appears to have generated inflectional variants, to the extent of including *concerninger*. This generally seems an advisable path towards improved consistency.

7 Improving Stop List Provision in OSS

Based on the analysis above, we propose strategies for better provision of stop lists in OSS:

Documentation Stop lists should be documented with their assumptions about tokenization and other limitations (e.g. genre). Documentation should also include information on provenance and how the list was built.

Dynamic Adaptation Stop lists can be adapted dynamically to match the NLP pipeline. For example, stop lists can be adjusted according to the tokenizer chosen by the user (e.g. through applying the tokenizer to the stop list); a word which is an inflectional variant of a stop word could also be removed

Quality Control The community should develop tools for identifying controversial terms in stop lists (e.g. words that are frequent in one corpus but infrequent in another), and to assist in assessing or mitigating incompleteness issues. For instance, future work could evaluate whether the nearest neighborhood of stop words in vector space can be used to identify incompleteness.

Tools for Automatic Generation A major limitation of published stop lists is their inapplicability to new domains and languages. We thus advocate language independent tools to assist in generating new lists, which could incorporate the quality control tools above.

8 Conclusion

Stop word lists are a simple but useful tool for managing noise, with ubiquitous support in natural language processing software. We have found that popular stop lists, which users often apply blindly, may suffer from surprising omissions and inclusions, or their incompatibility with particular tokenizers. Many of these issues may derive from generating stop lists using corpus statistics. We hence recommend better documentation, dynamically adapting stop lists during preprocessing, as well as creating tools for stop list quality control and automatically generating stop lists.

Acknowledgments

We thank Igor Brigadir for collecting and providing English-language stop word lists along with their provenance. We also thank Scikit-learn contributors for bringing these issues to our attention.

References

P. Daowadung and Y. H. Chen. 2012. Stop word in readability assessment of thai text. In *Proceedings of 2012 IEEE 12th International Conference on Advanced Learning Technologies*, pages 497–499.

Zelig Harris. 1954. Distributional structure. *Word*, 10(23):146–162.

Matthew Honnibal and Ines Montani. 2017. spaCy 2: Natural language understanding with bloom embeddings, convolutional neural networks and incremental parsing. *To appear*.

Christopher D. Manning, Prabhakar Raghavan, and Hinrich Schütze. 2008. *Introduction to Information Retrieval*. Cambridge University Press.

Jean-Baptiste Michel, Yuan Kui Shen, Aviva Presser Aiden, Adrian Veres, Matthew K. Gray, Joseph P. Pickett, Dale Hoiberg, Dan Clancy, Peter Norvig, Jon Orwant, Steven Pinker, Martin A. Nowak, and Erez Lieberman Aiden. 2011. Quantitative analysis of culture using millions of digitized books. *Science*, 331(6014):176–182.

Iadh Ounis, Gianni Amati, Vassilis Plachouras, Ben He, Craig Macdonald, and Douglas Johnson. 2005. Terrier information retrieval platform. In *Proceedings of the 27th European Conference on Advances in Information Retrieval Research*, pages 517–519.

Robert Parker, David Graff, Junbo Kong, Ke Chen, and Kazuaki Maeda. 2011. English Gigaword fifth edition LDC2011T07. Linguistic Data Consortium.

Fabian Pedregosa, Gaël Varoquaux, Alexandre Gramfort, Vincent Michel, Bertrand Thirion, Olivier Grisel, Mathieu Blondel, Peter Prettenhofer, Ron Weiss, Vincent Dubourg, Jake Vanderplas, Alexandre Passos, David Cournapeau, Matthieu Brucher, Matthieu Perrot, and Édouard Duchesnay. 2011. Scikit-learn: Machine learning in Python. *Journal of Machine Learning Research*, 12:2825–2830.

Radim Řehůřek and Petr Sojka. 2010. Software Framework for Topic Modelling with Large Corpora. In *Proceedings of the LREC 2010 Workshop on New Challenges for NLP Frameworks*, pages 45–50, Valletta, Malta. ELRA.

Mohammad Sadeghi and Jess Vegas. 2014. Automatic identification of light stop words for persian information retrieval systems. *Journal of Information Science*, 40(4):476–487.

Hassan Saif, Miriam Fernández, Yulan He, and Harith Alani. 2014. On stopwords, filtering and data sparsity for sentiment analysis of Twitter. In *Proceedings of the Ninth International Conference on Language Resources and Evaluation. Proceedings.*, pages 810–817.

Alexandra Schofield, Måns Magnusson, and David Mimno. 2017. Pulling out the stops: Rethinking stopword removal for topic models. In *Proceedings of the 15th Conference of the European Chapter of the Association for Computational Linguistics: Volume 2, Short Papers*, pages 432–436.

Benjamin Stone, Simon Dennis, and Peter J. Kwantes. 2010. Comparing methods for single paragraph similarity analysis. *Topics in Cognitive Science*, 3(1):92–122.

Feng Zou, Fu Lee Wang, Xiaotie Deng, Song Han, and Lu Sheng Wang. 2006. Automatic construction of chinese stop word list. In *Proceedings of the 5th WSEAS International Conference on Applied Computer Science*.

Texar: A Modularized, Versatile, and Extensible Toolbox for Text Generation

Zhiting Hu*, Zichao Yang, Haoran Shi, Bowen Tan, Tiancheng Zhao, Junxian He, Xiaodan Liang, Wentao Wang, Xingjiang Yu, Di Wang, Lianhui Qin, Xuezhe Ma, Hector Liu, Devendra Singh, Wangrong Zhu, Eric P. Xing
zhitingh@cs.cmu.edu*, Carnegie Mellon University, Petuum Inc.

Abstract

We introduce Texar, an open-source toolkit aiming to support the broad set of text generation tasks. Different from many existing toolkits that are specialized for specific applications (e.g., neural machine translation), Texar is designed to be highly flexible and versatile. This is achieved by abstracting the common patterns underlying the diverse tasks and methodologies, creating a library of highly reusable modules and functionalities, and enabling arbitrary model architectures and various algorithmic paradigms. The features make Texar particularly suitable for technique sharing and generalization across different text generation applications. The toolkit emphasizes heavily on extensibility and modularized system design, so that components can be freely plugged in or swapped out. We conduct extensive experiments and case studies to demonstrate the use and advantage of the toolkit.

1 Introduction

Text generation spans a broad set of natural language processing tasks that aim at generating natural language from input data or machine representations. Such tasks include machine translation (Bahdanau et al., 2014; Brown et al., 1990), dialog systems (Williams and Young, 2007; Serban et al., 2016), text summarization (Hovy and Lin, 1998; See et al., 2017), article writing (Wiseman et al., 2017), text paraphrasing and manipulation (Madnani and Dorr, 2010; Hu et al., 2017a), image captioning (Vinyals et al., 2015b; Karpathy and Fei-Fei, 2015), and more. Recent years have seen rapid progress of this active area in both academia and industry, especially with the adoption of modern deep learning approaches in many of the tasks. On the other hand, considerable research efforts are still needed to improve relevant techniques and enable real-world practical applications.

The variety of text generation tasks share many common properties and goals, e.g., to generate well-formed, grammatical and readable text, and to realize in the generation the desired information inferred from inputs. To this end, a few key models and algorithms are increasingly widely-used to empower the different applications, such as neural encoder-decoders (Sutskever et al., 2014), attentions (Bahdanau et al., 2014; Luong et al., 2015b), memory networks (Sukhbaatar et al., 2015), adversarial methods (Goodfellow et al., 2014; Hu et al., 2017b; Lamb et al., 2016), reinforcement learning (Ranzato et al., 2015; Bahdanau et al., 2016), as well as some optimization techniques, data preprocessing and result post-processing procedures, evaluations, etc.

It is therefore highly desirable to have an open-source platform that unifies the development of the diverse yet closely-related applications, backed with clean and consistent implementations of the core algorithms. Such a unified platform enables reuse of common components and functionalities, standardizes design, implementation, and experimentation, fosters reproducible research, and importantly, encourages technique sharing among different text generation tasks, so that an algorithmic advance originally developed for a specific task can quickly be evaluated and potentially generalized to many other tasks.

Though a few remarkable open-source toolkits have been developed, they have been largely designed for one or few specific tasks, especially neural machine translation (Britz et al., 2017; Klein et al., 2017; Neubig et al., 2018) and dialog related algorithms (Miller et al., 2017). This pa-

Proceedings of Workshop for NLP Open Source Software, pages 13–22
Melbourne, Australia, July 20, 2018.

per introduces *Texar*, a general-purpose text generation toolkit that aims to support most of the popular applications in the field, by providing researchers and practitioners a unified and flexible framework for building their models. Texar is built upon TensorFlow[1], a popular deep learning platform. Texar emphasizes on three key properties, namely, versatility, modularity, and extensibility.

- **Versatility**: Texar contains a wide range of features and functionalities for 1) arbitrary model architectures as a combination of encoders, decoders, discriminators, memories, and many other modules; and 2) different modeling and learning paradigms such as sequence-to-sequence, probabilistic models, adversarial methods, and reinforcement learning. Based on these, both workhorse and cutting-edge solutions to the broad spectrum of text generation tasks are either already included or can be easily constructed.

- **Modularity**: Texar is designed to be highly modularized, by decoupling solutions to diverse tasks into a set of highly reusable modules. Users can construct their model at a high conceptual level just like assembling LEGO bricks. It is convenient to plug in or swap out modules, configure rich options of each module, or even switch between distinct modeling paradigms. For example, switching between maximum likelihood learning and reinforcement learning involves only minimal code changes. Modularity makes Texar useful for fast prototyping, parameter tuning, and model experimentation.

- **Extensibility**: The toolkit provides interfaces of multiple functionality levels, ranging from simple Python-like configuration files to full library APIs. Users of different needs and expertise are free to choose different interfaces for appropriate programmability and internal accessibility. The library APIs are fully compatible with the native TensorFlow interfaces, which allows a seamless integration of user-customized modules, and enables the toolkit to take advantage of the vibrant open-source community by easily importing any external components as needed.

[1]https://www.tensorflow.org

Furthermore, Texar puts much emphasis on well-structured high-quality code of uniform design patterns and consistent styles, along with clean documentations and rich tutorial examples.

In the following, we provide details of the toolkit structure and design. To demonstrate the use of the toolkit and its advantages, we perform extensive experiments and cases studies, including generalizing the state-of-the-art machine translation model to multiple text generation tasks, investigating different algorithms for language modeling, and implementing composite neural architectures beyond conventional encoder-decoder for text style transfer. All are easily realized with the versatile toolkit.

Texar is under Apache license 2.0, and will be released very soon. Please check out `http://www.cs.cmu.edu/~zhitingh` for the release progress.

2 Structure and Design

In this section, we first provide an overview of the toolkit on its design principles and overall structures. We then present the detailed structure of Texar with running examples to demonstrate the key properties of the toolkit (sec 2.2-2.4).

Figure 1 shows the stack of main modules and functionalities in Texar. Building upon the lower level deep learning platform (TensorFlow), Texar provides a comprehensive set of building blocks for model construction, training, evaluation, and prediction. Texar is designed with the goals of *versatility, modularity, and extensibility* in mind. In the following, we first present the design principles that lead to the goals (sec 2.1), and describe the detailed structure of Texar with running examples to demonstrate the properties of the toolkit (sec 2.2-2.4).

2.1 The Design of Texar

The broad variation of the many text generation tasks and the fast-growing new models and algorithms have posed unique challenges to designing a versatile toolkit. We tackle the challenges through proper decomposition of the whole experimentation pipeline, extensive sets of modules to assemble freely, and user interfaces of varying abstract levels.

Pipeline Decomposition We begin with a high-level decomposition of model construction and learning pipeline. A deep neural model is typically

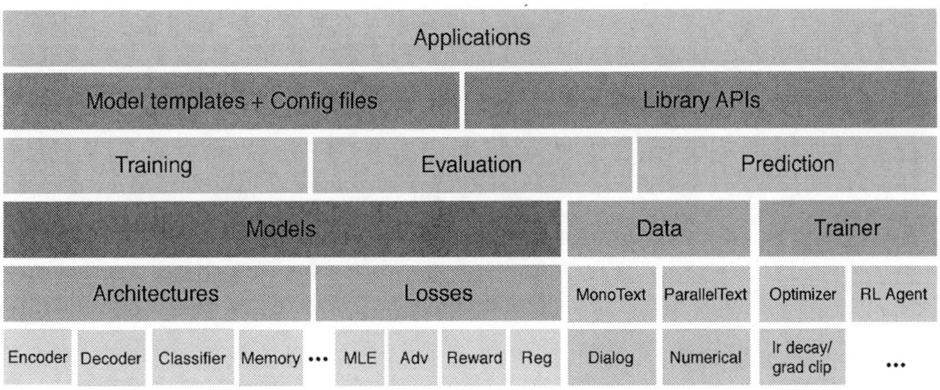

Figure 1: The stack of main modules and functionalities in Texar.

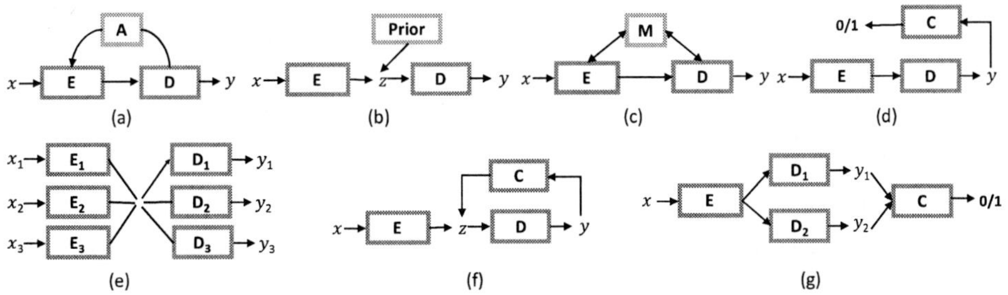

Figure 2: Example various model architectures in recent text generation literatures. E denotes encoder, D denotes decoder, C denotes classifier (i.e., binary discriminator). **(a)** The canonical encoder-decoder, sometimes with attentions A (Sutskever et al., 2014; Bahdanau et al., 2014; Luong et al., 2015b; Vaswani et al., 2017), or copy mechanisms (Gu et al., 2016; Vinyals et al., 2015a; Gulcehre et al., 2016); **(b)** Variational encoder-decoder (Bowman et al., 2015; Yang et al., 2017); **(c)** Encoder-decoder augmented with external memory (Sukhbaatar et al., 2015; Bordes et al., 2016); **(d)** Adversarial model using a binary discriminator C, with or without reinforcement learning (Liang et al., 2017; Zhang et al., 2017; Yu et al., 2017); **(e)** Multi-task learning with multiple encoders and/or decoders (Luong et al., 2015a; Firat et al., 2016); **(f)** Augmenting with cyclic loss (Hu et al., 2017a; Goyal et al., 2017); **(g)** Learning to align with adversary, either on samples y or hidden states (Lamb et al., 2016; Lample et al., 2017; Shen et al., 2017).

learned with the following abstract procedure:

$$\max_\theta \mathcal{L}(f_\theta, D) \tag{1}$$

where (1) f_θ is the model that defines the model architecture and the intrinsic inference procedure; (2) D is the data; (3) $\mathcal{L}$ is the losses to optimize; and (4) $\max$ denotes the optimization and learning procedure. Note that the above can have multiple losses imposed on different parts of components and parameters (e.g., generative adversarial networks (Goodfellow et al., 2014)). Texar is designed to properly decouple the four elements, and allow free combinations of them through uniform interfaces. Such design has underlay the strong modularity of the toolkit.

In particular, the decomposition of model architecture and inference (i.e., f_θ) from losses and learning has greatly improved the cleanness of the code structure and the opportunities for reuse. For example, a sequence decoder can focus solely on performing different decoding (inference) schemes, such as decoding with ground truths, and greedy, stochastic, or beam-search decoding, etc. Different learning algorithms then use different schemes as a subroutine in the learning procedure—for example, maximum likelihood learning uses decoding with ground truths (Mikolov et al., 2010), a policy gradient algorithm can use stochastic decoding (Ranzato et al., 2015), and an adversarial learning can use either the stochastic decoding for policy gradient-based updates (Yu et al., 2017) or the Gumbel-softmax reparameterized decoding (Jang et al., 2016) for direct gradient back-propagation.

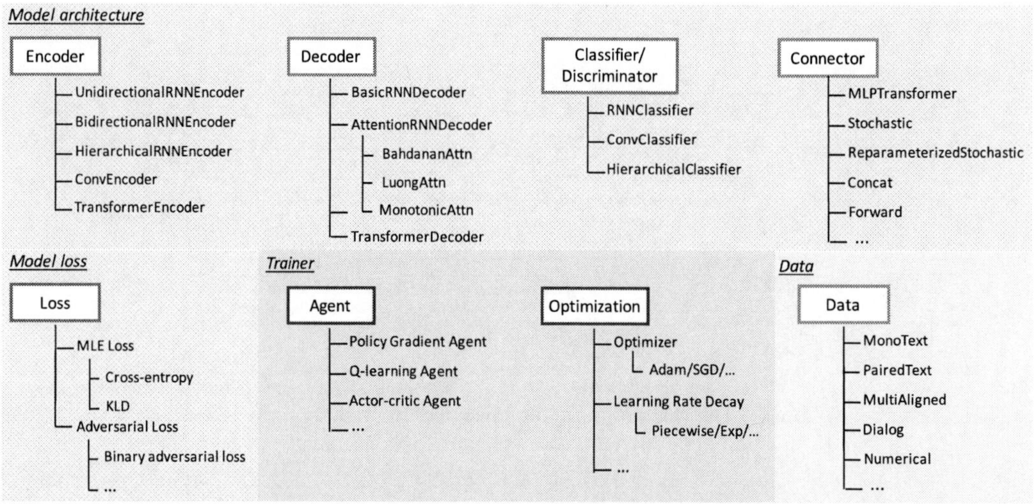

Figure 3: The catalog of a subset of modules for model construction and learning. Other modules, such as memory network modules, and those for evaluation and prediction, are omitted due to space limitations. More new modules are continuously added to the library.

With unified abstractions, the decoder and the learning algorithms need not know the implementation details of each other. This also enables convenient switch between different learning algorithms for the same model, by simply changing the inference scheme and connecting to the new learning module, without adapting the model architecture (see sec 2.3 for the example).

Modules Readily to Assemble The fast evolution of modeling and learning methodologies in the research field has led to sophisticated models that go beyond the canonical (attentive) sequence-to-sequence alike paradigms and introduce many new composite architectures. Figure 2 summarizes several model architectures recently used in the literature for different tasks. To versatilely support all these diverse approaches, we break down the complex models and extract a set of frequently-used modules (e.g., `encoders`, `decoders`, `classifiers`, etc). Figure 3 shows the catelog of a subset of modules. Crucially, Texar allows free concatenation between these modules in order to assemble arbitrary model architectures. Such concatenation can be done by directly interfacing two modules, or through an intermediate `connector` module that provides general, highly-usable functionalities of shape transformation, reparameterization (e.g., (Kingma and Welling, 2013; Jang et al., 2016)), sampling, and others.

User Interfaces It is critical for the toolkit to be flexible enough to allow construction of the simple or advanced models, while at the same time providing proper abstractions to relieve users from overly concerning about low-level implementations. To this end, Texar provides two types of user interfaces with different abstract levels: 1) Python-style configuration files that instantiate pre-defined model templates, and 2) a set of intuitive library APIs called in Python code. The former is simple, clean, straightforwardly understandable for non-expert users, and is widely adopted by other toolkits (Britz et al., 2017; Neubig et al., 2018; Klein et al., 2017), while the latter allows maximal flexibility, full access to internal states, and essentially unlimited customizability. Examples are provided in the following section.

2.2 Assemble Arbitrary Model Architectures

Figure 4 shows an example of specifying an attentive sequence-to-sequence model through either the YAML configuration file (left panel), or simple Python code (right panel), respectively.

- The configuration file passes hyperparameters to the model template which instantiates the model for subsequent training and evaluation (which are also configured through YAML). Text highlighted in blue in the figure specifies the names of modules to use. Module hyperparameters follow the module

```yaml
source_embedder: WordEmbedder
  dim: 300
encoder: UnidirectionalRNNEncoder
  rnn_cell:
    type: BasicLSTMCell
      num_units: 300
    num_layers: 1
    dropout:
      output_dropout: 0.5
      variational_recurrent: True
target_embedder: WordEmbedder
  dim: 300
decoder: AttentionRNNDecoder
  rnn_cell:
    type: BasicLSTMCell
      num_units: 300
    num_layers: 1
  attention:
    type: LuongAttention
connector: ZeroConnector
```

```python
# Read data
dataset = PairedTextData(data_hparams)
data = DataIterator(dataset).get_next()

# Encode
embedder = WordEmbedder(dataset.vocab_size, emb_dim)
encoder = UnidirectionalRNNEncoder(hparams=cell_hparams)
enc_outputs, _ = encoder(
  embedder(data['source_text_ids']), data['source_length'])

# Decode
decoder = AttentionRNNDecoder(
  memory=enc_outputs, attn_type='LuongAttention', hparams=cell_hparams)
outputs, length, _ = decoder(
  embedder(data['target_text_ids']), data['target_length']-1, mode='greedy_train')

# Loss
loss = sequence_sparse_softmax_cross_entropy(
  labels=data['target_text_ids'][:,1:], logits=outputs.logits, seq_length=length)
```

Figure 4: Two ways of specifying an attentive sequence-to-sequence model. **Left:** Snippet of an example YAML configuration file of the sequence-to-sequence model template. Only those hyperparameters that the user concerns are specified explicitly in the particular file, while the remaining many hyperparameters can be omitted and will take default values. **Right:** Python code assembling the sequence-to-sequence model, using the Texar library APIs. Modules are created as Python objects, and then can be called as functions to perform the main logic (e.g., decoding) of the module. (Other code such as optimization is omitted.)

names as children in the configuration hierarchy. Note that most of the hyperparameters have sensible default values, and users only have to specify a small subset of them. Hyperparameters taking default values can be omitted in the configuration file.

- The library APIs offer high-level function calls. Users are enabled to efficiently build desired pipelines at a high conceptual level, without worrying too much about the low-level implementations. Power users are also given the option to access the full internal states for native programming and low-level manipulations.

2.3 Plug-in and Swap-out Modules

Texar builds a shared abstraction of the broad set of text generation tasks, and creates highly reusable modules. It is thus very convenient to switch between different application contexts, or change from one modeling paradigm to another, by simply plugging in/swapping out a single or few modules, or even merely changing a configuration parameter, while keeping other parts of the modeling and training pipeline agnostic.

Figure 5 illustrates an example of switching between three major learning paradigms of an RNN decoder, i.e., maximum-likelihood based supervised learning, adversarial learning, and reinforcement learning, using the library APIs. Local modification of only few lines of code is enough to achieve such change. In particular, the same decoder is called with different decoding modes (e.g., `greed_train` and `greedy_infer`), and discriminator or reinforcement learning agent is added when needed, with simple API calls.

The convenient module replacement can be valuable for fast exploration of different algorithms for a specific task, or quick experimentation of an algorithm's generalization on different tasks.

2.4 Customize with Extensible Interfaces

With the aim of supporting the rapidly advancing research area of text generation, Texar emphasizes heavily on extensibility, and allows easy addition of customized or external modules through various interfaces, without editing the Texar codebase.

With the YAML configuration file, users can directly insert their own modules by providing the Python importing path to the module. For example, to use a externally implemented RNN cell in

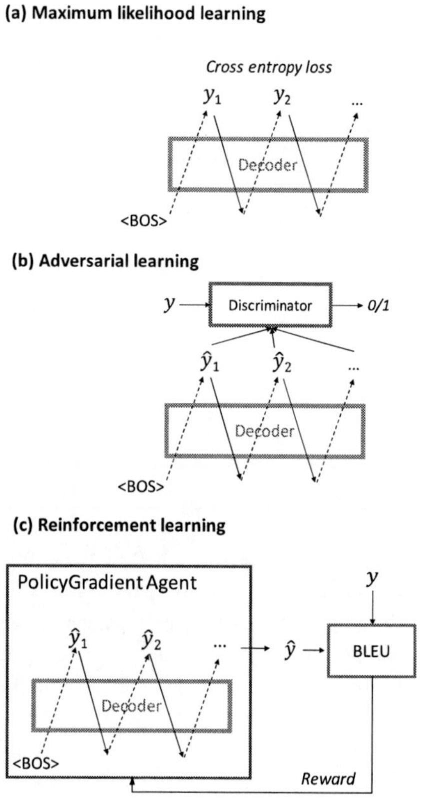


```
outputs, length, _ = decoder(
    embedder(data['target_text_ids']), data['target_length']-1, mode='greedy_train')

loss = sequence_sparse_softmax_cross_entropy(
    labels=data['target_text_ids'][:,1:], logits=outputs.logits, seq_length=length)
```

```
helper = GumbelSoftmaxTrainingHelper(
    start_tokens=[BOS]*batch_size, end_token=EOS, embedding=embedder)
outputs, _, _ = decoder(helper=helper)

discriminator = Conv1DClassifier(conv_hparams)
soft_embedder = SoftWordEmbedder(embedder.value)  # Share embedding

G_loss, D_loss = binary_adversarial_losses(
    embedder(data['target_text_ids']),
soft_embedder(softmax(outputs.logits)),discriminator)
```

```
agent = PolicyGradientAgent(
    policy=decoder,
    policy_kwargs={'start_tokens': [BOS]*batch_size, 'end_token': EOS,
                   'embedding': embedder, 'mode': 'greedy_infer'})

for i in range(STEPS):
    samples = agent.get_samples()
    rewards = BLEU(samples, data_batch['target_text_ids'])
    agent.perceive(samples, rewards)
```

Figure 5: Switching between the different learning paradigms of a decoder involves only modification of Line.14-19 in the right panel of Figure 4. In particular, the same decoder is called with different decoding modes (schemes), and the discriminator or reinforcement learning agent is added when needed, with simple API calls. **Left:** The module structure of each of the paradigms; **Right:** The respective code. For the adversarial learning in (b), the continuous Gumbel-softmax approximation (Jang et al., 2016) (with `GumbelSoftmaxTrainingHelper`) to the generated sample is used to enable gradient propagation from the discriminator to the decoder.

the sequence-to-sequence model encoder, one can simply change Lines.5-6 in the left panel of Figure 4 to the following:

```
5  type: path.to.MyCell
6      num_units: 300
7      some_new_arg: 123
8      ...
```

as long as the `MyCell` class is accessible by Python, and its interface is compatible to other parts of the model.

Incorporating customized modules with Texar library APIs is even more flexible and straightforward. As the library APIs are designed to be coherent with the native TensorFlow programming interfaces, any externally-defined modules can be seamlessly combined with Texar components to build arbitrary complex models and pipelines.

3 Experiments

We perform extensive experiments to demonstrate the use and advantage of Texar. In particular, we conduct case studies on *technique sharing* that is uniquely supported by our toolkit: (1) We deploy the state-of-the-art machine translation model on other tasks to study its generality, and obtain improved performance over previous methods; (2) We apply various model paradigms on the task of language modeling to compare the different methods. Besides, to further demonstrate the versatility of Texar, we show a case study on the newly-emerging task of text style transfer, which typically involves composite neural architectures beyond the conventional encoder-decoder.

Task: VAE language modeling			
Dataset	**Metrics**	**VAE-LSTM**	**VAE-Transformer**
Yahoo (Yang et al., 2017)	Test PPL	68.31	**61.26**
	Test NLL	337.36	**328.67**
PTB (Bowman et al., 2015)	Test PPL	105.27	**102.46**
	Test NLL	102.06	**101.46**

Table 1: Comparison of Transformer decoder and LSTM RNN decoder on VAE language modeling (Bowman et al., 2015). Test set perplexity (PPL) and sentence-level negative log likelihood (NLL) are evaluated (The lower the better).

3.1 One Technique on Many Tasks: Transformer

Transformer (Vaswani et al., 2017) is a recently developed model that achieves state-of-the-art performance on machine translation. Different from the widely-used attentive sequence-to-sequence models (Bahdanau et al., 2014), Transformer introduces a new *self-attention* technique in which each generated token attends to all previously generated tokens. It would be interesting to see how the technique generalizes to other text generation tasks beyond machine translation. We deploy the self-attention Transformer decoder on two tasks, namely, variational autoencoder (VAE) based language modeling (Bowman et al., 2015) and conversation generation (Serban et al., 2016).

The first task is to use the VAE model (Kingma and Welling, 2013) for language modeling. LSTM RNN has been widely-used in VAE for decoding sentences. We follow the experimental setting in previous work (Bowman et al., 2015; Yang et al., 2017), and test two models, one with the LSTM RNN decoder, and the other with the Transformer decoder. All other configurations (including the encoders) are the same in the two models. Changing the decoder in the whole experiment pipeline is easily achieved on Texar, thanks to the modularized design. Both the LSTM decoder and the Transformer decoder have around 6.3M free parameters to learn. Table 1 shows the results. We see that the VAE with Transformer decoder consistently improves over the VAE with conventional LSTM decoder.

The second task is to generate response given a conversation history. We use the popular hierarchical recurrent encoder-decoder model (HRED) (Serban et al., 2016) as the base model, which treats a conversation as a transduction task. The conversation history is seen as the source sequence and is modeled with a hierarchical encoder. Each utterance in the dialog history is first encoded with a first-level RNN. The resulting hidden states of the sequence of utterance are then encoded with a second-level RNN. We follow the experimental setting in (Zhao et al., 2017). In particular, the first-level RNN is set to be bidirectional and the second-level is unidirectional. Such configuration is easily implemented by setting the hyperparameters of the Texar `HierarchicalRNNEncoder`. Similar to the above task, we compare two models, one with an GRU RNN decoder as in the original work, and the other with an Transformer decoder. Table 2 shows the results. Again, we see that the Transformer model generalizes well to the conversation generation setting, and consistently outperforms the GRU RNN counterpart.

Task: Conversation generation		
Metrics	**HERD-GRU**	**HERD-Tnsfmr**
BLEU-3 prec	0.281	**0.289**
BLEU-3 recall	0.256	**0.273**
BLEU-4 prec	0.228	**0.232**
BLEU-4 recall	0.205	**0.214**

Table 2: Comparison of Transformer decoder and GRU RNN decoder on conversation generation within the HERD model (Bowman et al., 2015). The Switchboard data (Zhao et al., 2017) is used.

3.2 One Task with Many Techniques: Language Modeling

We next showcase how Texar can support investigation of diverse techniques on a single task. This can be valuable for research community to standardize experimental configurations and foster fair, reproducible comparisons. As as case study, we choose the standard language modeling task (Zaremba et al., 2014). Note that this is differ-

Models	Test PPL
LSTM RNN with MLE (Zaremba et al., 2014)	74.23
LSTM RNN with seqGAN (Yu et al., 2017)	74.12
Memory Network LM (Sukhbaatar et al., 2015)	94.82

Table 3: Comparison of the three models on the task of language modeling, using the PTB dataset (Zaremba et al., 2014).

Models	Accuracy	BLEU
Shen et al. (2017)	79.5	12.4
Shen et al. (2017) on Texar	82.5	13.0
Hu et al. (2017a) on Texar	**88.6**	**38.0**

Table 4: Text style transfer on the Yelp data (Shen et al., 2017). The first row is the original open-source implementation by the author (Shen et al., 2017). The subsequent two rows are Texar implementations of the two work.

ent from the VAE language modeling task above, due to different data partition strategies conventionally adopted in respective research lines.

We compare three models as shown in Table 3. The LSTM RNN trained with the maximum likelihood estimation (MLE) (Zaremba et al., 2014) is the most widely used model for language modeling, due to its simplicity and prominent performance. We use the exact same architecture as generator and setup a (seq)GAN (Yu et al., 2017) system to train the language model with adversarial learning. (The generator is pre-trained with MLE.) From Table 3 we see that adversarial learning does not improve the perplexity. This is partly because of the high variance of the policy gradient in seqGAN learning. Besides, test set perplexity is not a perfect metric for evaluating language modeling, though it is the most widely-used metrics in the field. We further evaluate a memory network-based language model (Sukhbaatar et al., 2015) which has the same number of free parameters (11M) with the LSTM RNN model. The test set perplexity is significantly higher than the LSTM RNNs, which is not unreasonable because LSTM RNN models are well studied for language modeling and a number of optimal modeling and optimization choices are already known.

3.3 Text Style Transfer

To further demonstrate the versatility of Texar for composing complicated model architectures, we next choose the the newly emerging task of text style transfer (Hu et al., 2017a; Shen et al., 2017). The task aims to manipulate the text of an input sentence to change from one style to another (e.g., from positive sentiment to negative), given only non-parallel training data of each style. The criteria is that the resulting sentence accurately entails the target style, while preserving the content and other properties well.

We use Texar to implement the models from both (Hu et al., 2017a) and (Shen et al., 2017), whose model architectures fall in the category (f) and (g) in Figure 2, respectively. Experimental settings mostly follow those in (Shen et al., 2017). Following previous setting, we use a pre-trained sentiment classifier to evaluate the transferred style accuracy. For evaluating how well the generated sentence preserves the original content, we measure the BLEU score between the generated sentence and the respective original one (The higher the better). Note that we do not mean to perform exhaustive evaluations of the methods, but instead aim to demonstrate the flexibility of the toolkit for implementing different composite model architectures beyond conventional encoder-decoder. Table 4 shows the results. Our re-implementation of (Shen et al., 2017) recovers and slightly surpasses the original results, while the implementation of (Hu et al., 2017a) provides the best performance in terms of the two metrics.

4 Related Work

Text generation is a broad research area with rapid advancement. Figure 2 summarizes some popular and emerging models used in the diverse contexts of the field. There are some existing toolkits that focus on tasks of neural machine translation and alike, such as Google Seq2seq (Britz et al., 2017) and Tensor2Tensor (Vaswani et al., 2018) on TensorFlow, OpenNMT (Klein et al., 2017) on (Py)Torch, XNMT (Neubig et al., 2018) on DyNet, and Nematus (Sennrich et al., 2017) on Theano, and MarianNMT (Junczys-Dowmunt et al., 2018) on C++. ParlAI (Miller et al., 2017) is a software platform specialized for dialog research. Differing from these task-specific toolkits, Texar aims to cover as many text generation tasks as possible. The goal of versatility poses unique challenges to the design. We combat the challenges through proper pipeline decomposition, ready-to-assemble modules, and user interfaces of varying abstract levels.

There are also libraries for general NLP applications (AllenAI; Pytorch; DMLC). With the focus on text generation, we provide a more comprehensive and readily-usable modules and functionalities to relevant tasks, enable users to efficiently build their pipelines at a high conceptual level without worrying too much on low-level details. Some platforms exist for specific types of algorithms, such as OpenAI Gym (Brockman et al., 2016), DeepMind Control Suite (Tassa et al., 2018), and ELF (Tian et al., 2017) for reinforcement learning in game environments. Texar has drawn inspirations from these toolkits when designing relevant specific algorithm supports.

5 Conclusion and Future Work

This paper has introduced Texar, a text generation toolkit that is designed to be versatile to support the broad set of applications and algorithms, to be modularized to enable easy replacement of any components, and to be extensible to allow seamless integration of any external modules. Features and functionalities will continue be added to the toolkit, including distributed model training, service deployment, more model building blocks, and more applications related to text generation or beyond. We invite researchers and practitioners to join and enrich the toolkit, and in the end help push forward the text generation research and applications together.

References

AllenAI. AllenNLP. Website: http://allennlp.org.

Dzmitry Bahdanau, Philemon Brakel, Kelvin Xu, Anirudh Goyal, Ryan Lowe, Joelle Pineau, Aaron Courville, and Yoshua Bengio. 2016. An actor-critic algorithm for sequence prediction. *arXiv preprint arXiv:1607.07086*.

Dzmitry Bahdanau, Kyunghyun Cho, and Yoshua Bengio. 2014. Neural machine translation by jointly learning to align and translate. *arXiv preprint arXiv:1409.0473*.

Antoine Bordes, Y-Lan Boureau, and Jason Weston. 2016. Learning end-to-end goal-oriented dialog. *arXiv preprint arXiv:1605.07683*.

Samuel R Bowman, Luke Vilnis, Oriol Vinyals, Andrew M Dai, Rafal Jozefowicz, and Samy Bengio. 2015. Generating sentences from a continuous space. *arXiv preprint arXiv:1511.06349*.

Denny Britz, Anna Goldie, Thang Luong, and Quoc Le. 2017. Massive exploration of neural machine translation architectures. *arXiv preprint arXiv:1703.03906*.

Greg Brockman, Vicki Cheung, Ludwig Pettersson, Jonas Schneider, John Schulman, Jie Tang, and Wojciech Zaremba. 2016. Openai gym. *arXiv preprint arXiv:1606.01540*.

Peter F Brown, John Cocke, Stephen A Della Pietra, Vincent J Della Pietra, Fredrick Jelinek, John D Lafferty, Robert L Mercer, and Paul S Roossin. 1990. A statistical approach to machine translation. *Computational linguistics*, 16(2):79–85.

DMLC. GluonNLP.

Orhan Firat, Kyunghyun Cho, and Yoshua Bengio. 2016. Multi-way, multilingual neural machine translation with a shared attention mechanism. *arXiv preprint arXiv:1601.01073*.

Ian Goodfellow, Jean Pouget-Abadie, Mehdi Mirza, Bing Xu, David Warde-Farley, Sherjil Ozair, Aaron Courville, and Yoshua Bengio. 2014. Generative adversarial nets. In *Advances in neural information processing systems*, pages 2672–2680.

Anirudh Goyal Alias Parth Goyal, Alessandro Sordoni, Marc-Alexandre Côté, Nan Ke, and Yoshua Bengio. 2017. Z-forcing: Training stochastic recurrent networks. In *Advances in Neural Information Processing Systems*, pages 6716–6726.

Jiatao Gu, Zhengdong Lu, Hang Li, and Victor OK Li. 2016. Incorporating copying mechanism in sequence-to-sequence learning. *arXiv preprint arXiv:1603.06393*.

Caglar Gulcehre, Sungjin Ahn, Ramesh Nallapati, Bowen Zhou, and Yoshua Bengio. 2016. Pointing the unknown words. *arXiv preprint arXiv:1603.08148*.

Eduard Hovy and Chin-Yew Lin. 1998. Automated text summarization and the summarist system. In *Proceedings of a workshop on held at Baltimore, Maryland: October 13-15, 1998*, pages 197–214. Association for Computational Linguistics.

Zhiting Hu, Zichao Yang, Xiaodan Liang, Ruslan Salakhutdinov, and Eric P Xing. 2017a. Toward controlled generation of text. In *International Conference on Machine Learning*.

Zhiting Hu, Zichao Yang, Ruslan Salakhutdinov, and Eric P Xing. 2017b. On unifying deep generative models. *arXiv preprint arXiv:1706.00550*.

Eric Jang, Shixiang Gu, and Ben Poole. 2016. Categorical reparameterization with gumbel-softmax. *arXiv preprint arXiv:1611.01144*.

Marcin Junczys-Dowmunt, Roman Grundkiewicz, Tomasz Dwojak, Hieu Hoang, Kenneth Heafield, Tom Neckermann, Frank Seide, Ulrich Germann, Alham Fikri Aji, Nikolay Bogoychev, Andr F. T. Martins, and Alexandra Birch. 2018. Marian: Fast neural machine translation in c++. *arXiv preprint arXiv:1804.00344*.

Andrej Karpathy and Li Fei-Fei. 2015. Deep visual-semantic alignments for generating image descriptions. In *Proceedings of the IEEE conference on computer vision and pattern recognition*, pages 3128–3137.

Diederik P Kingma and Max Welling. 2013. Auto-encoding variational bayes. *arXiv preprint arXiv:1312.6114*.

Guillaume Klein, Yoon Kim, Yuntian Deng, Jean Senellart, and Alexander M Rush. 2017. Opennmt: Open-source toolkit for neural machine translation. *arXiv preprint arXiv:1701.02810*.

Alex M Lamb, Anirudh Goyal Alias Parth Goyal, Ying Zhang, Saizheng Zhang, Aaron C Courville, and Yoshua Bengio. 2016. Professor forcing: A new algorithm for training recurrent networks. In *Advances In Neural Information Processing Systems*, pages 4601–4609.

Guillaume Lample, Ludovic Denoyer, and Marc'Aurelio Ranzato. 2017. Unsupervised machine translation using monolingual corpora only. *arXiv preprint arXiv:1711.00043*.

Xiaodan Liang, Zhiting Hu, Hao Zhang, Chuang Gan, and Eric P Xing. 2017. Recurrent topic-transition gan for visual paragraph generation. *CoRR, abs/1703.07022*, 2.

Minh-Thang Luong, Quoc V Le, Ilya Sutskever, Oriol Vinyals, and Lukasz Kaiser. 2015a. Multi-task sequence to sequence learning. *arXiv preprint arXiv:1511.06114*.

Minh-Thang Luong, Hieu Pham, and Christopher D Manning. 2015b. Effective approaches to attention-based neural machine translation. *arXiv preprint arXiv:1508.04025*.

Nitin Madnani and Bonnie J Dorr. 2010. Generating phrasal and sentential paraphrases: A survey of data-driven methods. *Computational Linguistics*, 36(3):341–387.

Tomáš Mikolov, Martin Karafiát, Lukáš Burget, Jan Černocký, and Sanjeev Khudanpur. 2010. Recurrent neural network based language model. In *Eleventh Annual Conference of the International Speech Communication Association*.

Alexander H Miller, Will Feng, Adam Fisch, Jiasen Lu, Dhruv Batra, Antoine Bordes, Devi Parikh, and Jason Weston. 2017. Parlai: A dialog research software platform. *arXiv preprint arXiv:1705.06476*.

Graham Neubig, Matthias Sperber, Xinyi Wang, Matthieu Felix, Austin Matthews, Sarguna Padmanabhan, Ye Qi, Devendra Singh Sachan, Philip Arthur, Pierre Godard, et al. 2018. Xnmt: The extensible neural machine translation toolkit. *arXiv preprint arXiv:1803.00188*.

Pytorch. QuickNLP.

Marc'Aurelio Ranzato, Sumit Chopra, Michael Auli, and Wojciech Zaremba. 2015. Sequence level training with recurrent neural networks. *arXiv preprint arXiv:1511.06732*.

Abigail See, Peter J Liu, and Christopher D Manning. 2017. Get to the point: Summarization with pointer-generator networks. *arXiv preprint arXiv:1704.04368*.

Rico Sennrich, Orhan Firat, Kyunghyun Cho, Alexandra Birch, Barry Haddow, Julian Hitschler, Marcin Junczys-Dowmunt, Samuel Läubli, Antonio Valerio Miceli Barone, Jozef Mokry, et al. 2017. Nematus: a toolkit for neural machine translation. *arXiv preprint arXiv:1703.04357*.

Iulian Vlad Serban, Alessandro Sordoni, Yoshua Bengio, Aaron C Courville, and Joelle Pineau. 2016. Building end-to-end dialogue systems using generative hierarchical neural network models.

Tianxiao Shen, Tao Lei, Regina Barzilay, and Tommi Jaakkola. 2017. Style transfer from non-parallel text by cross-alignment. In *Advances in Neural Information Processing Systems*, pages 6833–6844.

Sainbayar Sukhbaatar, Jason Weston, Rob Fergus, et al. 2015. End-to-end memory networks. In *Advances in neural information processing systems*, pages 2440–2448.

Ilya Sutskever, Oriol Vinyals, and Quoc V Le. 2014. Sequence to sequence learning with neural networks. In *Advances in neural information processing systems*, pages 3104–3112.

Yuval Tassa, Yotam Doron, Alistair Muldal, Tom Erez, Yazhe Li, Diego de Las Casas, David Budden, Abbas Abdolmaleki, Josh Merel, Andrew Lefrancq, et al. 2018. Deepmind control suite. *arXiv preprint arXiv:1801.00690*.

Yuandong Tian, Qucheng Gong, Wenling Shang, Yuxin Wu, and C Lawrence Zitnick. 2017. Elf: An extensive, lightweight and flexible research platform for real-time strategy games. In *Advances in Neural Information Processing Systems*, pages 2656–2666.

Ashish Vaswani, Samy Bengio, Eugene Brevdo, Francois Chollet, Aidan N Gomez, Stephan Gouws, Llion Jones, Łukasz Kaiser, Nal Kalchbrenner, Niki Parmar, et al. 2018. Tensor2tensor for neural machine translation. *arXiv preprint arXiv:1803.07416*.

Ashish Vaswani, Noam Shazeer, Niki Parmar, Jakob Uszkoreit, Llion Jones, Aidan N Gomez, Łukasz Kaiser, and Illia Polosukhin. 2017. Attention is all you need. In *Advances in Neural Information Processing Systems*, pages 6000–6010.

Oriol Vinyals, Meire Fortunato, and Navdeep Jaitly. 2015a. Pointer networks. In *Advances in Neural Information Processing Systems*, pages 2692–2700.

Oriol Vinyals, Alexander Toshev, Samy Bengio, and Dumitru Erhan. 2015b. Show and tell: A neural image caption generator. In *Computer Vision and Pattern Recognition (CVPR), 2015 IEEE Conference on*, pages 3156–3164. IEEE.

Jason D Williams and Steve Young. 2007. Partially observable markov decision processes for spoken dialog systems. *Computer Speech & Language*, 21(2):393–422.

Sam Wiseman, Stuart M Shieber, and Alexander M Rush. 2017. Challenges in data-to-document generation. *arXiv preprint arXiv:1707.08052*.

Zichao Yang, Zhiting Hu, Ruslan Salakhutdinov, and Taylor Berg-Kirkpatrick. 2017. Improved variational autoencoders for text modeling using dilated convolutions. *arXiv preprint arXiv:1702.08139*.

Lantao Yu, Weinan Zhang, Jun Wang, and Yong Yu. 2017. Seqgan: Sequence generative adversarial nets with policy gradient. In *AAAI*, pages 2852–2858.

Wojciech Zaremba, Ilya Sutskever, and Oriol Vinyals. 2014. Recurrent neural network regularization. *arXiv preprint arXiv:1409.2329*.

Yizhe Zhang, Zhe Gan, Kai Fan, Zhi Chen, Ricardo Henao, Dinghan Shen, and Lawrence Carin. 2017. Adversarial feature matching for text generation. *arXiv preprint arXiv:1706.03850*.

Tiancheng Zhao, Ran Zhao, and Maxine Eskenazi. 2017. Learning discourse-level diversity for neural dialog models using conditional variational autoencoders. *arXiv preprint arXiv:1703.10960*.

The ACL Anthology: Current State and Future Directions

Daniel Gildea
Department of Computer Science
University of Rochester
gildea@cs.rochester.edu

Min-Yen Kan
School of Computing
National University of Singapore
kanmy@comp.nus.edu.sg

Nitin Madnani
Educational Testing Service
Princeton, NJ
nmadnani@ets.org

Christoph Teichmann and **Martín Villalba**
Department of Language Science and Technology
Saarland University
villalba@coli.uni-saarland.de

Abstract

The Association of Computational Linguistic's Anthology is the open source archive, and the main source for computational linguistics and natural language processing's scientific literature. The ACL Anthology is currently maintained exclusively by community volunteers and has to be available and up-to-date at all times. We first discuss the current, open source approach used to achieve this, and then discuss how the planned use of Docker images will improve the Anthology's long-term stability. This change will make it easier for researchers to utilize Anthology data for experimentation. We believe the ACL community can directly benefit from the extension-friendly architecture of the Anthology. We end by issuing an open challenge of reviewer matching we encourage the community to rally towards.

1 Introduction

The ACL Anthology[1] is a service offered by the Association for Computational Linguistics (ACL) allowing open access to the proceedings of all ACL sponsored conferences and journal articles. As a community goodwill gesture, it also hosts third-party computational linguistics literature from sister organizations and their national venues. It offers both text and faceted search of the indexed papers, author-specific pages, and can incorporate third-party metadata and services that can be embedded within pages (Bysani and Kan, 2012). As of this paper, it hosts over 43,000 computational linguistics and natural language processing papers, along with their metadata. Over 4,500 daily requests are served by the Anthology. The code for the Anthology is available at https://github.com/acl-org/acl-anthology under the Creative Commons Attribution-NonCommercial-ShareAlike 3.0 International License[2]. Slightly different from the Anthology source code, ACL also licenses its papers with a more liberal license, supporting Creative Commons Attribution 4.0 International License[3], supporting liberal re-use of papers published with the ACL.

The maintenance of the code and the website is handled through volunteer efforts coordinated by the Anthology editor. Running a key service for the computational linguistics community that needs to be continuously available and updated frequently is one of the main issues in administering the Anthology.

We discuss this issue along with the challenges of running a large scale project on a volunteer basis and its resulting technical debt. As we look towards the future, previous research has shown that it can also be used as a data source to characterize the work and workings of the ACL community (Bird et al., 2008; Vogel and Jurafsky, 2012; Anderson et al., 2012). Extensions to the Anthology that build on this information could make the Anthology an even more valuable resource for the community. We will discuss two possibl eextensions – anonymous pre-prints and support for finding relevant submission reviewers by linking au-

[1] https://aclanthology.info/

[2] https://creativecommons.org/licenses/by-nc-sa/3.0/

[3] https://creativecommons.org/licenses/by/4.0/

Proceedings of Workshop for NLP Open Source Software, pages 23–28
Melbourne, Australia, July 20, 2018.

thors in the Anthology with their research interests and community connections. Beyond being useful in itself, work on such challenges has the potential to motivate the ACL community to further support the Anthology.

2 Current State of the Anthology

The ACL Anthology was proposed as a project to the ACL Executive by Steven Bird at the 2001 ACL conference and first launched in 2002, with a second version developed in 2012, commissioned by the ACL committee. Steven Bird also served as the first editor of the anthology from 2002 to 2007, a post which Min-Yen Kan took over in 2008 and continues to fill as of today. The Anthology provides access to papers in Portable Document Format (PDF) as well as the associated metadata in multiple formats (e.g., BIBTEX and Endnote). For recent papers, authors can also opt include data, notes and open-source software, and may provide Digital Object Identifiers (DOIs) for permalinking the citations within their papers.

The technology behind the current version is detailed in Table 1. As a community project, daily administration and development is handled by volunteers. However, to tackle larger problems with the Anthology which require a more focused effort, the ACL committee has solicited paid assistance. Hosting and bandwidth for the Anthology has historically been provided by universities free of charge. It was hosted at the National University of Singapore until the spring of 2017, when it was migrated to its current home at Saarland University. In the future, hosting duties are planned to fall under the umbrella of the ACL itself, unifying all services under `https://www.aclweb.org/portal/`.

Framework	Ruby on Rails
Search engine	Solr
Database	PostgreSQL
Web server (Prod./Test)	Nginx / Jetty
Operating System	Debian GNU-Linux

Table 1: Tech stack for the ACL Anthology.

The most important task is the importing, indexing and provisioning of newly accepted papers from recent conference proceedings and journal issues. The original Anthology defined an XML format for simple bibliographic metadata, which has been extended to support the more recent features of associated software, posters, videos and datasets that accompany the scholarly publications. Providing the XML for new materials is an semi-automated process that is largely integrated with the various mechanisms for managing ACL conference submissions and printed proceedings. It is straightforward for ACL events that utilize the licensed START conference management software[4], as an established software pipeline builds upon the artefacts used for creation of the final publications themselves. After the accepted papers are finalized, START produces an archive file of camera-ready PDF files and author-provided metadata such as the title, author list, and abstract for each paper. These files are processed by a set of scripts in START maintained by ACL publication chairs in order to assign page numbers to papers, and to produce a PDF proceedings volume for each conference complete with a table of contents, author index, and other front matter. These scripts also produce bibliographic information that are programmatically transformed into the ACL Anthology's XML format. The Anthology is then updated with the author-provided PDFs and the XML metadata. For importing journal articles and venues not using the START submission system, additional manual work is necessary to construct the Anthology XML. Sanity checks and some manual curation is also necessary to deal with issues such as character encodings and accents in names, multipart family names, and so on. This pipeline has reached a point of high efficiency, but may need to be adapted if the ACL ever considers it necessary to integrate with a different service for conference organization.

3 Running the Anthology as a Community Project

Since the Anthology is not tied to a specific research project or institution, contributors that work on Anthology-related system administration and development tasks have been recruited in response to calls for volunteers at the main ACL conferences. In contrast, new features have been developed by researchers using the ACL Anthology as a resource in their own work, unconnected with the daily operation of the Anthology. Such research deliverables include, for example, the creation of a corpus of research papers (Bird et al., 2008), an author citation network (Radev et al., 2013) or a

[4] `https://www.softconf.com/`

faceted search engine (Schäfer et al., 2012; Buitelaar et al., 2014). These factors, in combination with the multiple, changing responsibilities and shifting research interests of community members, mean that new volunteers join and leave the Anthology team in unpredictable and sporadic patterns. Preserving knowledge about the Anthology's operational workflow is thus one of the most important challenges for the Anthology.

The Anthology editor has played a key role ensuring the continuity of the entire project. This position has so far always been filled for multiple years, longer than the normal time frame for an ACL officer. The role has been critical in ensuring a smooth transition between volunteers, at the cost of a long term with a heavy workload and a potential single point of failure. In order to tackle both issues, there is currently a concerted effort to improve the documentation of all tasks related to maintaining the Anthology.

As the ACL community and its publishing needs continue to grow, the ACL Executive is considering commercial support for publishing. While this may be suitable for help with daily operations, we strongly advocate the continuation and promotion of a closely-knit volunteer group for development. Passing the responsibilities for the Anthology to a commercial devoid who has no intrinsic interest in the Anthology's scientific contents may end up poorly.

4 Future Proofing the Anthology

All code, documentation, bug reports, and feature requests are hosted at `https://github.com/acl-org/acl-anthology`, along with instructions detailing the steps required to set up an instance of the Anthology and keep it updated with proceedings for new conferences. These instructions have been verified and updated using test builds. We began with the initial documentation provided by experienced contributors to the project and the original developer. New volunteers were then asked to set up and update a new instance of the Anthology on a new server while communicating with more experienced contributors. The documentation was expanded and updated based on the problems and questions encountered during this process. The resulting documentation will likely reduce the learning curve for new volunteers and will make their recruitment easier. It will also make it easier to migrate the Anthology to new servers when the hosting arrangement changes or to create mirrors. The latter is an important future task for the Anthology in order to ensure that alternatives are available if the main Anthology server experiences any downtime.

The current implementation of the Anthology has been extended over the years with minor improvements to functionality and bug fixes. The core code has remained mostly intact from its original version and has proved to be robust and reliable. However, fearing the introduction of bugs and instability (Spolsky, 2000), the maintainers chose to keep the software working in its current state for as long as the technology would allow it, and focus their resources instead on features that would help the community with their research and publication efforts.

This choice is not without its drawbacks. One key problem is the deprecation of dependencies with time. For example, Ruby 2.0 is no longer available in Debian repositories, and SSL support no longer compiles against it by default. These problems can be seen as indicators that delaying upgrades might not be feasible for much longer. Where possible, deprecated libraries are replaced with newer versions. This is the case for the database, web server, and the Java interpreter, all of which have been replaced with little extra effort. When a new version of a library breaks backwards compatibility, the software is either upgraded or frozen in its current version. Ruby (frozen at `2.0.0-p353` via RVM) and Solr are both examples of the latter, with detailed documented instructions to replicate the software environment.

In addition to the production Anthology site, a second version is kept on low-cost cloud servers for testing purposes. This copy has proven useful for testing step-by-step instructions, since rolling back the server to a clean state requires neither authorization nor downtime. It is also used as a staging area, and to do trial imports of new proceedings and for volunteer training.

Security is another major concern: older dependencies increase exposure to unpatched bugs. The Anthology currently does not collect or store personal data, rendering the consequences of a data breach modest. A compromised server, however, presents not only a risk for the maintainers (service downtime, unauthorized applications) but for the community at large, due to the large number of researchers who could be exposed to malicious scripts. While the former puts the goodwill of the hosting institution at risk, the latter would affect a large portion of the ACL community.

To tackle issues with outdated software, the Anthology volunteer group is working on making the entire Anthology available via a Docker image (Matthias and Kane, 2015). Docker provides a virtualized environment (also known as a *container*) in which software can be run but where, unlike a virtual machine, the underlying operating system resources can be used directly. Containers are typically stateless, allowing system administrators to add and restart services with minimum friction. Hosting a mirror of the Anthology with Docker containers abstracts away the relatively complex server setup and makes it easier to tackle dependency problems independently from future mirror deployments. As a result, hosting institutions can apply their own internal security policies, and the community can benefit from the added robustness via a larger network of mirrors. Development versions of this image are already available at `https://github.com/acl-org/anthology-docker`. When an instance of this Docker container is started, it first downloads all the data necessary to run the Anthology, inclusive of the metadata and source publications (PDF files) for all proceedings hosted within the Anthology. The resulting Anthology instance is a peer of the production site, but completely independent. This makes it possible for member institutions and even interested individual members to easily provide a mirror or experiment with the data in the Anthology.

Freezing software versions has proven useful to keep stability under control, improve documentation practices, and implement long-requested features like search engine indexing. This does not preclude a full software upgrade from being part of our development roadmap. With better test coverage and expanded consistency checks in place, we expect the first successful upgrade tests to be within our reach in the near future.

Docker containers and temporary servers also show great promise for researchers. An isolated, easy-to-replicate software environment reduces friction in transferring tools between researchers usually caused by incompatible software, simplifies the replication of experiments, and limits the data loss due to software bugs. A container-like approach specifying complete environments can also help in distributing code and general research within the community (e.g., CodaLab[5] as used in SemEval competitions). In the future, best practices within the community may encourage researchers to program and experiment within Docker images to aid reproducibility.

The Anthology is currently stable and supports its current, intended use. However, to ensure that the ACL Anthology continues fulfilling its key roles, we call on the members of the ACL to help with both its operational and development goals:

- hosting mirrors of the Anthology and developing policy for mirror management;
- adding and indexing new publications to the Anthology;
- maintaining and updating the code underlying the Anthology;
- extending the capabilities of the Anthology to help tackle new challenges facing the ACL.

5 Challenges for the Anthology

Maintaining community buy-in for the Anthology is necessary to ensure its future. This is best assured by extending the Anthology with useful capabilities that align with research efforts. This is crucially enabled by the liberal licensing scheme that the ACL employs for the publications to empower end users. Research on the history and structure of the NLP community based on this data has already been undertaken (Anderson et al., 2012; Vogel and Jurafsky, 2012).

Anonymous Pre-prints. A current challenge needing attention is the result of the increasing popularity of pre-prints and their role in promoting scientific progress. However, such pre-print systems are not anonymous, interfering with the well-documented gains that author-blinded publications help in combating bias. Through membership polls and subcommitee study, the ACL executive has adopted a recent set of guidelines upholding the value of double-blinded submissions (ACL Executive Committee, 2017).

One solution would be the use of anonymous pre-prints as an option for authors. Currently two ways of implementing this have been discussed: as a collaboration with an existing pre-print service such as arXiv[6] or through hosting pre-prints

[5]`https://worksheets.codalab.org/`

[6]`https://arxiv.org/`

directly within the Anthology. While the latter option would be a challenge to the Anthology – requiring increased resources both for monitoring the submissions and for scaling the system architecture to a larger and less controlled inflow of papers – but could result in better community control of the process, and a greater awareness and feeling of co-ownership of the Anthology and its data among ACL members.

Reviewer Matching. One key problem with scientific conference and journal organization is in finding suitable reviewers for the peer review process, which is also a key problem for ACL.[7] We believe that we can leverage the ACL Anthology data to support conference organizers in the assignment of potential peer reviewers. There has been a substantial growth in the number of submissions to the main ACL conferences in recent years (Barzilay, 2017), and the ACL has been active in supporting automated approaches to solve the problem (Stent and Ji, 2018) such as the Toronto Paper Matching System (TPMS) (Charlin and Zemel, 2013). However, data for judging the fit between a reviewer and submitted papers are available in the Anthology; i.e., a reviewer's interests and expertise as encoded in their previous publications. Mining and representing such information directly from the Anthology, where data about potential reviewers is already available, makes it unnecessary to upload papers to an external platform, mitigating current low response rates. Measuring overlap between reviewer interests and a submitted paper, based on the reviewer's previous publications, is a problem that the NLP community is ideally suited to solve. Furthermore, the information generated by such a tool could serve conference chairs and journal editors when considering how much weight to assign to a review from specific reviewers. The data required for building such a tool would be both the text and metadata from every submitted paper. While some metadata is already accessible within the Anthology, clean textual content of papers would need to be harvested from the source PDF files, which currently has been partially achieved. (Bird et al., 2008) suggests that the text can generally be extracted using standard tools, with additional processing only necessary for a small fraction of the data. We are aware that clean textual data from the Anthology archives is current on-going interest being investigated by a number of NLP/CL teams within the community.

[7]As intimated through internal discussions with the ACL executive committee.

If such a solution were to be implemented, it would be in the interest of the entire community to have the Anthology maintainers integrate it directly into the Anthology, with support from the original implementers. This has been a problem in the past, where attempts to extend the capabilities of the Anthology with more detailed search and annotation (Schäfer et al., 2011, 2012) were spun off as independent systems to start with and have still not become part of the Anthology service.

We note that these two challenges are synergistically solved. Solving the first challenge will provide the submissions' source text within the Anthology framework and promote better coupling for the second challenge of reviewer matching.

6 Conclusion

The ACL Anthology is a key resource for researchers in the NLP community. We have described the software engineering and maintenance work that goes on behind-the-scenes in order for the Anthology to serve its purpose. This includes ingestion of new papers, maintenance of the Anthology codebase, and the social aspects of recruiting volunteers for this work. The task of training future volunteers and ensuring Anthology uptime is likely to become easier due to improved documentation and simplified server set-up. However, recruitment of new volunteers continues to be an issue.

We invite all community members to download the Anthology images for experimentation, not only for the challenge of automated reviewer assignment, but also for other use cases based on their own research interests. We hope that open challenges and the tasks associated with extending the usefulness of the Anthology will motivate more community members to take interest and become and familiar with its inner workings. We extend an open invitation to anyone interested in the Anthology to get in touch with the members of the team. Our current needs are focused on system administration, software development, database management, and Docker integration, but any kind of experience is welcome.

References

ACL Executive Committee. 2017. Acl policies for submission, review and citation. https://www.aclweb.org/adminwiki/index.php?title=ACL_Policies_for_Submission,_Review_and_Citation. [Online; accessed 05-April-2018].

Ashton Anderson, Dan McFarland, and Dan Jurafsky. 2012. Towards a Computational History of the ACL: 19802008. In *Proceedings of the ACL Special Workshop 2012 on Rediscovering 50 years of Discoveries*.

Regina Barzilay. 2017. Statistics on Submissions and Status Update. https://acl2017.wordpress.com/2017/02/15/statistics-on-submissions-and-status-update/. [Online; accessed 05-April-2018].

Steven Bird, Robert Dale, Bonnie Dorr, Bryan Gibson, Mark Joseph, Min-Yen Kan, Dongwon Lee, Brett Powley, Dragomir Radev, and Yee Fan Tan. 2008. The ACL Anthology Reference Corpus: A Reference Dataset for Bibliographic Research in Computational Linguistics. In *Language Resources and Evaluation Conference (LREC 08)*, Marrakesh, Morocco.

Paul Buitelaar, Georgeta Bordea, and Barry Coughlan. 2014. Hot topics and schisms in NLP: Community and trend analysis with saffron on ACL and LREC proceedings. In *9th Edition of Language Resources and Evaluation Conference (LREC2014)*.

Praveen Bysani and Min-Yen Kan. 2012. Integrating User-Generated Content in the ACL Anthology. In *Proceedings of the ACL Special Workshop 2012 on Rediscovering 50 years of Discoveries*.

Laurent Charlin and Richard S. Zemel. 2013. The Toronto Paper Matching System: An automated paper-reviewer assignment system. In *ICML Workshop on Peer Reviewing and Publishing Models (PEER)*.

Karl Matthias and Sean P. Kane. 2015. *Docker: Up & Running*. O'Reilly Media, Inc.

Dragomir R. Radev, Pradeep Muthukrishnan, Vahed Qazvinian, and Amjad Abu-Jbara. 2013. The ACL anthology network corpus. *Language Resources and Evaluation Journal*.

Ulrich Schäfer, Bernd Kiefer, Christian Spurk, Jörg Steffen, and Rui Wang. 2011. The ACL Anthology Searchbench. In *Proceedings of the ACL-HLT 2011 System Demonstrations*.

Ulrich Schäfer, Jonathon Read, and Stephan Oepen. 2012. The ACL Anthology Searchbench. In *Proceedings of the ACL Special Workshop 2012 on Rediscovering 50 years of Discoveries*.

Joel Spolsky. 2000. Things You Should Never Do, Part I. https://www.joelonsoftware.com/2000/04/06/things-you-should-never-do-part-i. [Online; accessed 29-March-2018].

Amanda Stent and Heng Ji. 2018. A Review of Reviewer Assignment Methods. https://naacl2018.wordpress.com/2018/01/28/a-review-of-reviewer-assignment-methods. [Online; accessed 29-March-2018].

Adam Vogel and Dan Jurafsky. 2012. He Said, She Said: Gender in the ACL Anthology. In *Proceedings of the ACL Special Workshop 2012 on Rediscovering 50 years of Discoveries*.

The risk of sub-optimal use of Open Source NLP Software: UKB is inadvertently state-of-the-art in knowledge-based WSD

Eneko Agirre
IXA NLP group
UPV/EHU

Oier López de Lacalle
IXA NLP group
UPV/EHU

Aitor Soroa
IXA NLP group
UPV/EHU

{e.agirre,oier.lopezdelacalle,**a.soroa**}@ehu.eus

Abstract

UKB is an open source collection of programs for performing, among other tasks, knowledge-based Word Sense Disambiguation (WSD). Since it was released in 2009 it has been often used out-of-the-box in sub-optimal settings. We show that nine years later it is the state-of-the-art on knowledge-based WSD. This case shows the pitfalls of releasing open source NLP software without optimal default settings and precise reproducibility instructions.

1 Introduction

The release of open-source Natural Language Processing (NLP) software has been key to make the field progress, as it facilitates other researchers to build upon previous results and software easily. It also allows easier reproducibility, allowing for sound scientific progress. Unfortunately, in some cases, it can also allow competing systems to run the open-source software out-of-the-box with sub-optimal parameters, specially in fields where there is no standard benchmark and new benchmarks (or new versions of older benchmarks) are created.

Once a paper reports sub-optimal results for a NLP software, newer papers can start to routinely quote the low results from the previous study. Finding a fix to this situation is not easy. The authors of the software can contact the authors of the more recent papers, but it is usually too late for updating the paper. Alternatively, the authors of the NLP software can try to publish a new paper with updated results, but there is usually no venue for such a paper, and, even if published, it might not be noticed in the field.

In this paper we want to report such a case in Word Sense Disambiguation (WSD), where the original software (UKB) was released with sub-optimal default parameters. Although the accompanying papers did contain the necessary information to obtain state-of-the-art results, the software did not contain step-by-step instructions, or end-to-end scripts for optimal performance. This case is special, in that we realized that the software is able to attain state-of-the-art results also in newer datasets, using the same settings as in the papers.

The take-away message for open-source NLP software authors is that they should not rely on other researchers reading the papers with care, and that it is extremely important to include, with the software release, precise instructions and optimal default parameters, or better still, end-to-end scripts that download all resources, perform any necessary pre-processing and reproduce the results.

The first section presents UKB and WSD, followed by the settings and parameters. Next we present the results and comparison to the state-of-the-art. Section 5 reports some additional results, and finally, we draw the conclusions.

2 WSD and UKB

Word Sense Disambiguation (WSD) is the problem of assigning the correct sense of a word in a context (Agirre and Edmonds, 2007). Traditionally, supervised approaches have attained the best results in the area, but they are expensive to build because of the need of large amounts of manually annotated examples. Alternatively, knowledge based approaches rely on lexical resources such as WordNet, which are nowadays widely available in many languages (Bond and Paik, 2012)[1]. In particular, graph-based approaches represent the knowledge base as a graph, and apply several well-known graph analysis algorithms to perform WSD.

[1]http://compling.hss.ntu.edu.sg/omw/

Proceedings of Workshop for NLP Open Source Software, pages 29–33
Melbourne, Australia, July 20, 2018.

UKB is a collection of programs which was first released for performing graph-based Word Sense Disambiguation using a pre-existing knowledge base such as WordNet, and attained state-of-the-art results among knowledge-based systems when evaluated on standard benchmarks (Agirre and Soroa, 2009; Agirre et al., 2014). In addition, UKB has been extended to perform disambiguation of medical entities (Agirre et al., 2010), named-entities (Erbs et al., 2012; Agirre et al., 2015), word similarity (Agirre et al., 2009) and to create knowledge-based word embeddings (Goikoetxea et al., 2015). All programs are open source[2,3] and are accompanied by the resources and instructions necessary to reproduce the results. The software is quite popular, with 60 stars and 26 forks in github, as well as more than eight thousand direct downloads from the website since 2011. The software is coded in C++ and released under the GPL v3.0 license.

When UKB was released, the papers specified the optimal parameters for WSD (Agirre and Soroa, 2009; Agirre et al., 2014), as well as other key issues like the underlying knowledge-base version, specific set of relations to be used, and method to pre-process the input text. At the time, we assumed that future researchers would use the optimal parameters and settings specified in the papers, and that they would contact the authors if in doubt. The default parameters of the software were not optimal, and the other issues were left under the users responsibility.

The assumption failed, and several papers reported low results in some new datasets (including updated versions of older datasets), as we will see in the following sections.

3 UKB parameters and setting for WSD

When using UKB for WSD, the main parameters and settings can be classified in five main categories. For each of those we mention the best options and the associated UKB parameter when relevant (in italics), as taken from (Agirre and Soroa, 2009; Agirre et al., 2014):

- Pre-processing of input text. When running UKB for WSD, one needs to define which window of words is to be used as context to initialize the random walks. One option is to take just the sentence, but given that in some cases the sentences are very short, better results are obtained when considering previous and following sentences. The procedure in the original paper repeated the extension procedure until the total length of the context is at least 20 words[4].

- Knowledge base relations. When performing WSD for English, UKB uses WordNet (Fellbaum, 1998) as a knowledge base. WordNet comes in various versions, and usually UKB performs best when using the same version the dataset was annotated with. Besides regular WordNet relations, gloss relations (relations between synsets appearing in the glosses) have been shown to be always helpful.

- Graph algorithm. UKB implements different graph-based algorithms and variants to perform WSD. These are the main ones:
  ppr_w2w: apply personalized PageRank for each target word, that is, perform a random walk in the graph personalized on the word context. It yields the best results overall, at the cost of being more time consuming that the rest.
  ppr: same as above, but apply personalized PageRank to each sentence only once, disambiguating all content words in the sentence in one go. It is thus faster that the previous approach, but obtains worse results.
  dfs: unlike the two previous algorithms, which consider the WordNet graph as a whole, this algorithm first creates a subgraph for each context, following the method first presented in Navigli and Lapata (2010), and then runs the PageRank algorithm over the subgraph. This option represents a compromise between *ppr_w2w* and *ppr*, as it faster than than the former while better than the latter.

- The PageRank algorithm has two parameters which were set as follows: number of iterations of power method (*prank_iter*) 30, and damping factor (*prank_damping*) 0.85.

- Use of sense frequencies (*dict_weight*). Sense frequencies are a valuable piece of informa-

[2]`http://ixa2.si.ehu.eus/ukb`

[3]`https://github.com/asoroa/ukb`

[4]The number 20 was initial arbitrarily set in the experiments of (Agirre and Soroa, 2009) somewhat arbitrarily, and never changed afterwards.

	All	S2	S3	S07	S13	S15
UKB (this work)	**67.3**	68.8	66.1	53.0	**68.8**	**70.3**
UKB (elsewhere)†‡	57.5	60.6	54.1	42.0	59.0	61.2
Chaplot and Sakajhutdinov (2018) ‡	66.9	**69.0**	**66.9**	55.6	65.3	69.6
Babelfy (Moro et al., 2014)†	65.5	67.0	63.5	51.6	66.4	70.3
MFS	65.2	66.8	66.2	55.2	63.0	67.8
Basile et al. (2014)†	63.7	63.0	63.7	**56.7**	66.2	64.6
Banerjee and Pedersen (2003)†	48.7	50.6	44.5	32.0	53.6	51.0

Table 1: F1 results for knowledge-based systems on the (Raganato et al., 2017a) dataset. Top rows show conflicting results for UKB. † for results reported in (Raganato et al., 2017a), ‡ for results reported in (Chaplot and Sakajhutdinov, 2018). Best results in bold. S2 stands for Senseval-2, S3 for Senseval-3, S07 for Semeval-2007, S13 for Semeval-2013 and S15 for Semeval-2015.

	All	S2	S3	S07	S13	S15
Yuan et al. (2016)	**71.5**	**73.8**	**71.8**	63.5	**69.5**	**72.6**
Raganato et al. (2017b)	69.9	72.0	69.1	**64.8**	66.9	71.5
Iacobacci et al. (2016)†	69.7	73.3	69.6	61.1	66.7	70.4
Melamud et al. (2016)†	69.4	72.3	68.2	61.5	67.2	71.7
IMS (Zhong and Ng, 2010)†	68.8	72.8	69.2	60.0	65.0	69.3

Table 2: F1 results for supervised systems on the (Raganato et al., 2017a) dataset. † for results reported in (Raganato et al., 2017a). Best results in bold. Note that (Raganato et al., 2017b) used S07 for development.

tion that describe the frequencies of the associations between a word and its possible senses. The frequencies are often derived from manually sense annotated corpora, such as Semcor (Miller et al., 1993). We use the sense frequency accompanying Wordnet, which, according to the documentation, "represents the decimal number of times the sense is tagged in various semantic concordance texts". The frequencies are smoothed adding one to all counts (*dict_weight_smooth*). The sense frequency is used when initializing context words, and is also used to produce the final sense weights as a linear combination of sense frequencies and graph-based sense probabilities. The use of sense frequencies with UKB was introduced in (Agirre et al., 2014).

4 Comparison to the state-of-the-art

We evaluate UKB on the recent evaluation dataset described in (Raganato et al., 2017a). This dataset comprises five standard English all-words datasets, standardized into a unified format with gold keys in WordNet version 3.0 (some of the original datasets used older versions of WordNet). The dataset contains $7,253$ instances of $2,659$ different content words (nouns, verbs, adjectives and adverbs). The average ambiguity of the words in the dataset is of 5.9 senses per word. We report F1, the harmonic mean between precision and recall, as computed by the evaluation code accompanying the dataset.

The two top rows in Table 1 show conflicting results for UKB. The first row corresponds to UKB ran with the settings described above. The second row was first reported in (Raganato et al., 2017a). As the results show, that paper reports a suboptimal use of UKB. In more recent work, Chaplot and Sakajhutdinov (2018) take up that result and report it in their paper as well. The difference is of nearly 10 absolute F1 points overall.[5] This decrease could be caused by the fact that Raganato et al. (2017a) did not use sense frequencies.

In addition to UKB, the table also reports the best performing knowledge-based systems on this dataset. Raganato et al. (2017a) run several well-known algorithms when presenting their datasets. We also report (Chaplot and Sakajhutdinov, 2018),

[5]Note that the UKB results for S2, S3 and S07 (62.6, 63.0 and 48.6 respectively) are different from those in (Agirre et al., 2014), which is to be expected, as the new datasets have been converted to WordNet 3.0 (we confirmed experimentally that this is the sole difference between the two experiments).

	All	S2	S3	S07	S13	S15
Single context sentence						
ppr_w2w	66.9	**69.0**	65.7	53.9	67.1	69.9
dfs_ppr	65.2	67.5	65.6	53.6	62.7	68.2
ppr	65.5	67.5	**66.5**	**54.7**	63.3	67.4
ppr_w2w_{nf}	60.2	63.7	55.1	42.2	63.5	63.8
ppr_{nf}	57.1	60.5	53.8	41.3	58.0	61.4
dfs_{nf}	58.7	63.3	52.8	40.4	61.6	62.5
One or more context sentences ($\#words \geq 20$)						
ppr_w2w	**67.3**	68.8	66.1	53.0	**68.8**	**70.3**
ppr	65.6	67.5	66.4	54.1	64.0	67.8
dfs	65.7	67.9	65.9	54.5	64.2	68.1
ppr_w2w_{nf}	60.4	64.2	54.8	40.0	64.5	64.5
ppr_{nf}	58.6	61.3	54.9	42.2	60.9	62.9
dfs_{nf}	59.1	62.7	54.4	39.3	62.8	62.2

Table 3: Additional results on other settings of UKB. nf subscript stands for "no sense frequency". Top rows use a single sentence as context, while the bottom rows correspond to extended context (cf. Sect. 3). Best results in bold.

the latest work on this area, as well as the most frequent sense as given by WordNet counts (see Section 3). The table shows that UKB yields the best overall result. Note that Banerjee and Pedersen (2003) do not use sense frequency information.

For completeness, Table 2 reports the results of supervised systems on the same dataset, taken from the two works that use the dataset (Yuan et al., 2016; Raganato et al., 2017b). As expected, supervised systems outperform knowledge-based systems, by a small margin in some of the cases.

5 Additional results

In addition to the results of UKB using the setting in (Agirre and Soroa, 2009; Agirre et al., 2014) as specified in Section 3, we checked whether some reasonable settings would obtain better results. Table 3 shows the results when applying the three algorithms described in Section 3, both with and without sense frequencies, as well as using a single sentence for context or extended context. The table shows that the key factor is the use of sense frequencies, and systems that do not use them (those with a nf subscript) suffer a loss between 7 and 8 percentage points in F1. This would explain part of the decrease in performance reported in (Raganato et al., 2017a), as they explicitly mention that they did not activate the use of sense frequencies in UKB.

The table also shows that extending the context is mildly effective. Regarding the algorithm, the table confirms that the best method is *ppr_w2w*, followed by the subgraph approach (*dfs*) and *ppr*.

6 Conclusions

This paper presents a case where an open-source NLP software was used with suboptimal parameters by third parties. UKB was released with suboptimal default parameters, and although the accompanying papers did describe the necessary settings for good results on WSD, bad results were not prevented. The results using the settings described in the paper on newly released datasets show that UKB is the best among knowledge-based WSD algorithms.

The take-away message for open-source NLP software authors is that they should not rely on other researchers reading the papers with care, and that it is extremely important to include, with the software release, precise instructions and optimal default parameters, or better still, end-to-end scripts that download all resources, perform any necessary pre-processing and reproduce the results. UKB now includes in version 3.1 such end-to-end scripts and the appropriate default parameters.

Acknowledgements

This research was partially supported by the Spanish MINECO (TUNER TIN2015-65308-C5-1-R and MUSTER PCIN-2015-226) and the UPV/EHU (excellence research group).

References

E. Agirre and P. Edmonds. 2007. *Word Sense Disambiguation: Algorithms and Applications*, 1st edition. Springer Publishing Company, Incorporated.

E. Agirre, O. Lopez de Lacalle, and A. Soroa. 2014. Random walks for knowledge-based word sense disambiguation. *Computational Linguistics*, 40(1):57–88.

E. Agirre and A. Soroa. 2009. Personalizing PageRank for Word Sense Disambiguation. In *Proceedings of 14th Conference of the European Chapter of the Association for Computational Linguistics*, Athens, Greece.

E. Agirre, A. Soroa, E. Alfonseca, K. Hall, J. Kravalova, and M. Pasca. 2009. A Study on Similarity and Relatedness Using Distributional and WordNet-based Approaches. In *Proceedings of annual meeting of the North American Chapter of the Association of Computational Linguistics (NAAC)*, Boulder, USA.

E. Agirre, A. Soroa, and M. Stevenson. 2010. Graph-based word sense disambiguation of biomedical documents. *Bioinformatics*, 26:2889–2896.

Eneko Agirre, Ander Barrena, and Aitor Soroa. 2015. Studying the wikipedia hyperlink graph for relatedness and disambiguation. In *ArXiv repository*.

Satanjeev Banerjee and Ted Pedersen. 2003. Extended gloss overlaps as a measure of semantic relatedness. In *Proceedings of the 18th International Joint Conference on Artificial Intelligence*, IJCAI'03, pages 805–810, San Francisco, CA, USA. Morgan Kaufmann Publishers Inc.

Pierpaolo Basile, Annalina Caputo, and Giovanni Semeraro. 2014. An enhanced lesk word sense disambiguation algorithm through a distributional semantic model. In *COLING*, pages 1591–1600. ACL.

Francis Bond and Kyonghee Paik. 2012. A survey of wordnets and their licenses. In *GWC 2012 6th International Global Wordnet Conference*.

D.S. Chaplot and R. Sakajhutdinov. 2018. Knowledge-based Word Sense Disambiguation using Topic Models. In *AAAI*.

Nicolai Erbs, Eneko Agirre, Aitor Soroa, Ander Barrena, Ugaitz Etxebarria, Iryna Gurevych, and Torsten Zesch. 2012. Ukp-ubc entity linking at tac-kbp. In *Text Analysis Conference, Knowledge Base Population*.

Christiane Fellbaum, editor. 1998. *WordNet: an electronic lexical database*. MIT Press.

Josu Goikoetxea, Eneko Agirre, and Aitor Soroa. 2015. Random walks and neural network language models on knowledge bases. In *Proceedings of the Annual Meeting of the North American chapter of the Association of Computational Linguistics (NAACL HLT 2015), pages 1434-1439. ISBN: 978-1-937284-73-2. Denver (USA)*.

Ignacio Iacobacci, Mohammad Taher Pilehvar, and Roberto Navigli. 2016. Embeddings for word sense disambiguation: An evaluation study. In *Proceedings of the 54th Annual Meeting of the Association for Computational Linguistics (Volume 1: Long Papers)*, pages 897–907, Berlin, Germany. Association for Computational Linguistics.

Oren Melamud, Jacob Goldberger, and Ido Dagan. 2016. context2vec: Learning generic context embedding with bidirectional lstm. In *CoNLL*.

George A. Miller, Claudia Leacock, Randee Tengi, and Ross T. Bunker. 1993. A semantic concordance. In *Proceedings of the workshop on Human Language Technology*, HLT '93, pages 303–308, Stroudsburg, PA, USA. Association for Computational Linguistics.

A. Moro, A. Raganato, and R. Navigli. 2014. Entity linking meets word sense disambiguation: a unified approach. *Transactions of the Association of Computational Linguistics*, 2:231–244.

R. Navigli and M. Lapata. 2010. An Experimental Study of Graph Connectivity for Unsupervised Word Sense Disambiguation. *IEEE Transactions on Pattern Analysis and Machine Intelligence*, 32(4):678–692.

Alessandro Raganato, Jose Camacho-Collados, and Roberto Navigli. 2017a. Word Sense Disambiguation: A Unified Evaluation Framework and Empirical Comparison. In *Proceedings of the 15th Conference of the European Chapter of the Association for Computational Linguistics: Volume 1, Long Papers*, pages 99–110. Association for Computational Linguistics.

Alessandro Raganato, Claudio Delli Bovi, and Roberto Navigli. 2017b. Neural sequence learning models for word sense disambiguation. In *Proceedings of the 2017 Conference on Empirical Methods in Natural Language Processing*, pages 1156–1167, Copenhagen, Denmark. Association for Computational Linguistics.

Dayu Yuan, Julian Richardson, Ryan Doherty, Colin Evans, and Eric Altendorf. 2016. Semi-supervised word sense disambiguation with neural models. In *Proceedings of COLING 2016, the 26th International Conference on Computational Linguistics: Technical Papers*, pages 1374–1385. The COLING 2016 Organizing Committee.

Zhi Zhong and Hwee Tou Ng. 2010. It makes sense: A wide-coverage word sense disambiguation system for free text. In *Proceedings of the ACL 2010 System Demonstrations*, ACLDemos '10, pages 78–83, Stroudsburg, PA, USA. Association for Computational Linguistics.

Baseline: A Library for Rapid Modeling, Experimentation and Development of Deep Learning Algorithms targeting NLP

Daniel Pressel, Sagnik Ray Choudhury, Brian Lester, Yanjie Zhao and Matt Barta

Interactions Digital Roots

{dpressel, schoudhury, blester, yzhao, mbarta}@interactions.com

Abstract

We introduce Baseline: a library for reproducible deep learning research and fast model development for NLP. The library provides easily extensible abstractions and implementations for data loading, model development, training and export of deep learning architectures. It also provides implementations for simple, high-performance, deep learning models for various NLP tasks, against which newly developed models can be compared. Deep learning experiments are hard to reproduce, Baseline provides functionalities to track them. The goal is to allow a researcher to focus on model development, delegating the repetitive tasks to the library.

1 Introduction

Deep Neural Network models (DNNs) now dominate the NLP literature. However, the immense progress comes with some issues. Often the research is not reproducible. Sometimes the code is not open source. Other times, available implementations fail to match the reported performance. When training DNNs, even simple baselines can take a lot of time and resources to reach peak performance (Melis et al., 2017). Additionally, a simple, canonical way to evaluate new models is lacking. Institutional pressures exist to show large relative gains in papers (Armstrong et al., 2009). As a result, new models are often compared with weak baselines.

When software is provided, it is common for authors to provide the source code as a standalone application. These projects include data processing, data cleaning, model training, and evaluation code, yielding an error-prone and time-consuming development process. A complete library should be used to automate the mundane portions of development, allowing a researcher to focus on model improvements. Also, it should be easy to compare the results of a new model across various hyper-parameter configurations and strong baselines.

To solve these problems, we have developed **Baseline**[1]. It has three components.

Core: An object-oriented Python library for rapid development of deep learning algorithms. Core provides extensible base classes for common components in a deep learning architecture (data loading, model development, training, evaluation, and export) in TensorFlow and PyTorch, with experimental support for DyNet. In addition, it provides strong, deep learning baselines for four fundamental NLP tasks – Classification, Sequence Tagging, Sequence-to-Sequence Encoder-Decoders and Language Modeling. Many NLP problems can be seen as variants of these tasks. For example, Part of Speech (POS) Tagging, Named Entity Recognition (NER) and Slot-filling are all Sequence Tagging tasks, Neural Machine Translation (NMT) is typically modeled as an Encoder-Decoder task. An end-user can easily implement a new model and delegate the rest to the library.

MEAD: A library built on Core for fast Modeling, Experimentation And Development. MEAD contains driver programs to run experiments from JSON or YAML configuration files to completely control the reader, trainer, model, and hyper-parameters.

XPCTL: A command-line interface to track experimental results and provide access to a global leaderboard. After running an experiment through MEAD, the results and the logs are committed to a database. Several commands are provided to show the best experimental results under various constraints.

The workflow for developing a deep learning

[1] `https://github.com/dpressel/baseline`

Proceedings of Workshop for NLP Open Source Software, pages 34–40
Melbourne, Australia, July 20, 2018.

model using Baseline is simple: 1. Map the problem to one of the existing tasks using a <task, dataset> tuple, eg., NER on CoNLL 2003 dataset is a <tagger task, conll> 2. Use the existing implementations in **Core** or extend the base model class to create a new architecture; 3. Define a configuration file in **MEAD** and run an experiment. 4. Use **XPCTL** to compare the result with the previous experiments, commit the results to the leaderboard database and the model files to a persistent storage if desired.

Additionally, the base models provided by the library can be exported from saved checkpoints directly into TensorFlow Serving[2] for deployment in a production environment. the framework can be run within a Docker container to reduce the installation complexity and to isolate experiment configurations and variants. It is open-sourced, actively maintained by a team of core developers and accepts public contributions. While some components from the library can be used for generic machine learning and computer vision tasks, the primary focus of Baseline is NLP: currently the data loaders, models and evaluation codes are provided for NLP tasks only.

2 Related Work

Baseline is not a general toolkit for deep learning (Bergstra et al., 2011; Abadi et al., 2016; Chen et al., 2015; Neubig et al., 2017a; Paszke et al., 2017). Rather, it *builds on* TensorFlow (Abadi et al., 2016), PyTorch (Paszke et al., 2017) and DyNet (Neubig et al., 2017b). Any model used in Baseline will be written in one of the supported, underlying frameworks. Popular NLP libraries such as Stanford CoreNLP (Manning et al., 2014) or nltk (Loper and Bird, 2002) provide abstractions and implementations for different algorithms in a complete NLP architecture: from basic (tokenization) to advanced (semantic parsing) tasks. Baseline serves a complimentary purpose: the models developed here can be used in these architectures.

To the best of our knowledge, two other software efforts have similar goals: AllenNLP (Gardner et al., 2017) and CodaLab [3]. AllenNLP is most similar to our work: like Baseline, it provides data and method APIs for common NLP problems and a modular and extensible experimentation framework. The key abstractions of AllenNLP are focused on data representation and conversion. This makes the model development easy for semantic understanding tasks. In Baseline, the key abstraction is an NLP "task", making it very generic. Both Baseline and AllenNLP allow running experiments from JSON configuration files, but AllenNLP currently does not provide utilities to store these configurations or results in a database in order to "track" an experiment (section 4). AllenNLP is built on PyTorch, where Baseline supports PyTorch, TensorFlow and DyNet and has a flexible design to support other frameworks over time. The development of Baseline initially began in early 2016, prior to the development of AllenNLP, and the libraries have been developed in parallel. The idea of reproducible experimentation for machine learning was introduced by CodaLab, but it does not provide abstractions and baseline implementations specific to deep learning or NLP, nor does it provide an extensible architecture with reusable components for building and exploring new deep learning models.

3 Baseline: Core

The top-level module provides base classes for data loading and evaluation. The data loader reads common file formats for classification, CONLL-formatted IOB files for sequence tagging, TSV and standard parallel corpora files for Neural Machine Translation and text files for language modeling. The data is masked and padded as necessary. It is also shuffled, sorted and batched such that data vectors in each batch have similar lengths. For sequence tagging problems, the loader supports multiple user-defined features. Also, the reader supports common formats for pretrained embeddings. The library also supports common data cleaning procedures.

The top-level module provides model base classes for the four tasks mentioned previously. The lower-level modules provide at least one implementation for each task in both TensorFlow and PyTorch. For most tasks, DyNet implementations are also available. The library provides methods to calculate standard evaluation metrics including precision, recall, F1, average loss, and perplexity. It also provides high-level utility support for common architecture layers and paradigms such as attention, highway and skip connections. The default trainer supports multiple optimizers, early

[2] https://www.tensorflow.org/serving/
[3] http://codalab.org/

stopping, and various learning rate schedules.

Model architecture development is a common use-case for a researcher. The library is designed to make this process extremely easy. In Baseline, a new model is known as an *addon*, which is a dynamically loaded module containing user-defined code. The addon code should be written as a python file in the format <task-name>_<model-name>.py and should be available to the python interpreter (the location should be in the system PYTHONPATH variable). The model should be written in one of the supported deep learning frameworks. If the task is not one of the existing ones, the mead.Task class has to be extended. The methods create_model() and load_model() have to be overridden and exposed as shown in listing 1. To run the code, the model-name has to be passed as an argument to the trainer program. The default trainer and data loaders can be overriden in a similar way.

The following sections describe the tasks and the implemented algorithms.

Classification: For Classification, the input is typically a sequence of words. These words are represented with word embeddings, a composition of character embeddings, or both. Sentences are represented as a combination of word representations using pooling or the final output of an RNN. A final linear layer and softmax is used for classification (Kim, 2014; Collobert et al., 2011). Baseline currently supports these models and an MLP built on pre-trained word embeddings with max-over-time pooling or mean-pooling (Neural Bag of Words) (Kalchbrenner et al., 2014).

Sequence Tagging: For Sequence Tagging, input words are represented similarly to the method used for Classification. State-of-the-art tagging is typically performed using bi-directional LSTMs (BLSTMs) with a Conditional Random Field (CRF) layer on top to promote global coherence (Lample et al., 2016; Ma and Hovy, 2016; Peters et al., 2017). Two common variants of this architecture differ primarily in the treatment of character-composition, either using a convolutional (Dos Santos and Zadrozny, 2014) or BLSTM layer (Ling et al., 2015). The convolutional composition approach is simpler and faster, yet achieves performances similar to the BLSTM (Reimers and Gurevych, 2017). Baseline implements this model and makes the CRF layer optional. It improves this model using multiple parallel convolutional filters and residual connections. It also supports multiple features such as gazetteer information.

Encoder-Decoders: Encoder-Decoder frameworks are used for Machine Translation, Image Captioning, Automatic Speech Recognition, and many other applications. Sequence-to-Sequence models are Encoder-Decoder architectures with an input sequence and an output sequence, which typically differ in length. We implement the most common version of this architecture for NLP: a stack of recurrent layers for the encoder and the decoder. We support multiple types of RNNs, including GRUs and LSTMs, as well as bidirectional encoders, multiple mechanisms of bridging the input encoder to the output decoder, and the most common types of global attention. We also provide a beam-search decoder for testing the model on standard tasks such as NMT.

Language Modeling: Language Modeling with RNNs operate at the word level or at the character level. Most baseline implementations use word-based models following (Zaremba et al., 2014) but character-compositional models (Kim et al., 2016; Józefowicz et al., 2016) may significantly reduce the number of parameters. Baseline has implementations for both word-based models and character-compositional models, closely following the model architecture of Kim et al. (2016).

3.1 Dataset and Results

Table 3.1 summarizes the TensorFlow implementation results. The PyTorch results are equivalent. Detailed results and hyper-parameter configurations are maintained in the library codebase.

For **Classification**, we use three public datasets: 2-class Stanford Sentiment Treebank (SST2) (Socher et al., 2013), TREC QA (Voorhees and Tice, 2000), and DBpedia (Auer et al., 2007). The **Sequence Tagger** has been tested on several problems including NER (CoNLL 2003 (Sang and Meulder, 2003), wnut17 (Derczynski et al., 2017) datasets), POS Tagging (Twitter dataset (Gimpel et al., 2011): TwPOS) and Slot Filling (ATIS dataset (Dahl et al., 1994)). The CRF layer is critical for NER but not necessary for ATIS and the Twitter POS corpus. For **Language Modeling**, our model improves on Zaremba et al. (2014) using pre-trained word embeddings. The state-of-the-art for Language Modeling has changed sig-

```
def create_model(embeddings, labels, **kwargs):
        return MyModel.create(embeddings, labels, **kwargs)

def load_model(modelname, **kwargs):
        return MyModel.load(modelname, **kwargs)
```

Listing 1: Methods to override and expose in a user-defined model

nificantly since our implementation and we anticipate releasing a new baseline model in the future (Yang et al., 2017). Our **Encoder-Decoder** model is tested on English-Vietnamese Translation Task on TED tst2013 corpus (Cettolo et al., 2015) and achieves strong results.

Apart from these base models, we provide implementations of more advanced models that can demonstrate the software architecture and provide a stepping stone for researchers developing their own models. Some of these implementations show better results than the existing state of the art. For example, using pre-trained ELMo embeddings from TensorFlow Hub (Peters et al., 2018), our tagger has 42.19% F1 for the wnut17 dataset, which is better than the last reported highest score (41.86%) on the dataset (Derczynski et al., 2017). The repository [4] is updated continually with the list of available implementations.

4 MEAD and XPCTL

DNNs are heavily dependent on hyper-parameter tuning, yet many papers do not report the exact hyper-parameters. This often leads to non-reproducible research. To solve this problem, we have developed **MEAD** and **XPCTL** to track hyper-parameters, model architecture, and results of a deep learning experiment.

MEAD: MEAD provides a driver program that runs experiments from a configuration file (in JSON/YAML format). We define a problem as a <task, dataset> tuple. For any task, the configuration file should contain 1. The dataset name, 2. Embedding type, 3. Reader type, 4. Model type, 5. Model hyper-parameters (number of layers, convolution filter size), 6. Training parameters (number of epochs, optimizers, optimizer specific parameters, patience for early stopping), 7. Pre-processing information. Reasonable default values are provided where possible. Thus, the whole experiment including hyper-parameters is uniquely identified by the sha1 hash of the configuration file. An experiment produces comprehensive logs including step-wise loss on the training data and task-specific metrics on the development and test sets. The reporting hooks support popular visualization frameworks including Tensorboard logging and Visdom. The model is persisted after each epoch, or, when early-stopping is enabled, whenever the model improves on the target development metric. The persisted model can be used to restart the training process or perform inference.

XPCTL: XPCTL (experiment control) can be used to track and compare the results with the previous ones by providing a command line interface to a database. The current implementation supports common databases including MongoDB, PostgreSQL and SQLite. The existing base classes can be extended to support other databases if needed. The configuration file, logs, and results can be stored in the database through a command. XPCTL also helps to maintain a leaderboard for these tasks. The results for a problem (<task, dataset>) can be sorted by any evaluation metric, filtered for particular users and limited by a number. Configuration files can be downloaded and the model files can be stored in a persistent storage location using the same utility.

The current implementation delegates the database creation and maintenance to the user. In future, we plan to maintain a global database accessible to all users. The user can also have her own local database, and push to the global leaderboard as needed. XPCTL will provide command line utilities for this purpose.

5 Exporting Models

DNNs can be deployed within a model serving framework such as **TensorFlow Serving**, a high-performance and highly scalable deployment architecture. All of the baseline implementations have exporters, though some customization may be required for user-defined models, for which we provide interfaces. The exporter transforms the model to include pre-processing and service-

[4] `https://github.com/dpressel/baseline/tree/master/python/addons`

Problem	Dataset	Algorithm	Metric	Score
Tagging	ConLL 2003	CNN-BLSTM-CRF	F1	90.88
	wnut17	CNN-BLSTM-CRF		39.19
	TwPOS	CNN-BLSTM		88.91
	ATIS	CNN-BLSTM		96.74
Classification	SST2	CNN	accuracy	87.9
		LSTM		87.1
	TREC-QA	CNN		93.2
		LSTM		91.8
	DBpedia	CNN		99.05
		LSTM		98.95
Language Modelling	PTB	RNN	perplexity	77.22
Encoder-Decoder	TED tst2013	Seq2Seq	BLEU	25.21

Table 1: Results for TensorFlow implementations in Baseline

consumable output.

6 Conclusion and Future Work

We have presented Baseline, a library for reproducible experimentation and fast development of DNN models in NLP. Our goal is to help automate the frustrating parts of the process of model development and deployment to allow researchers to focus on innovation. The library is currently used in a production environment for various problems, attesting to the fact that it is suitable for a complete research-to-deployment pipeline. Currently, the library has implementations for many strong baseline models which we will continue to update and improve as the state-of-the-art changes. Future versions of the software will attempt to improve the development process further by assisting with automatic parameter tuning and model selection, support for more deep learning frameworks, improved visualization, and a simpler cross-platform deployment mechanism.

Acknowledgments

We thank Patrick Haffner, Nick Ruiz and John Chen for their valuable feedback. Funding for this research was provided by Interactions LLC.

References

Martín Abadi, Paul Barham, Jianmin Chen, Zhifeng Chen, Andy Davis, Jeffrey Dean, Matthieu Devin, Sanjay Ghemawat, Geoffrey Irving, Michael Isard, Manjunath Kudlur, Josh Levenberg, Rajat Monga, Sherry Moore, Derek Gordon Murray, Benoit Steiner, Paul A. Tucker, Vijay Vasudevan, Pete Warden, Martin Wicke, Yuan Yu, and Xiaoqiang Zheng. 2016. Tensorflow: A system for large-scale machine learning. In *12th USENIX Symposium on Operating Systems Design and Implementation, OSDI 2016, Savannah, GA, USA, November 2-4, 2016.*, pages 265–283.

Timothy G. Armstrong, Justin Zobel, William Webber, and Alistair Moffat. 2009. Relative significance is insufficient: Baselines matter too.

Sören Auer, Christian Bizer, Georgi Kobilarov, Jens Lehmann, Richard Cyganiak, and Zachary Ives. 2007. Dbpedia: A nucleus for a web of open data. In *Proceedings of the 6th International The Semantic Web and 2Nd Asian Conference on Asian Semantic Web Conference*, ISWC'07/ASWC'07, pages 722–735, Berlin, Heidelberg. Springer-Verlag.

James Bergstra, Olivier Breuleux, Frederic Bastien, Pascal Lamblin, Razvan Pascanu, Guillaume Desjardins, Joseph Turian, David Warde-Farley, and Yoshua Bengio. 2011. Theano: A cpu and gpu math compiler in python. In *Proc. 9th Python in Science Conf*, volume 1.

Mauro Cettolo, Jan Niehues, Sebastian Stüker, Luisa Bentivogli, Roldano Cattoni, and Marcello Federico. 2015. The iwslt 2015 evaluation campaign. In *IWSLT 2015, International Workshop on Spoken Language Translation*.

Tianqi Chen, Mu Li, Yutian Li, Min Lin, Naiyan Wang, Minjie Wang, Tianjun Xiao, Bing Xu, Chiyuan Zhang, and Zheng Zhang. 2015. Mxnet: A flexible and efficient machine learning library for heterogeneous distributed systems. *CoRR*, abs/1512.01274.

Ronan Collobert, Jason Weston, Lon Bottou, Michael Karlen, Koray Kavukcuoglu, and Pavel P. Kuksa. 2011. Natural language processing (almost) from scratch. *Journal of Machine Learning Research*, 12:2493–2537.

Deborah A. Dahl, Madeleine Bates, Michael Brown adn William Fisher, Kate Hunicke-Smith, David Pallett, Christine Pao, Alexander Rudnicky, Elizabeth Shriberg, John S. Garofolo, Jonathan G. Fiscus, Denise Danielson, Enrico Bocchieri, Bruce Buntschuh, Beverly Schwartz, Sandra Peters, Robert Ingria, Robert Weide, Yuzong Chang, Eric Thayer, Lynette Hirschman, Joe Polifroni, Bruce Lund, Goh Kawai, Tom Kuhn, and Lew Norton. 1994. Atis3 training data ldc94s19.

Leon Derczynski, Eric Nichols, Marieke van Erp, and Nut Limsopatham. 2017. Results of the WNUT2017 shared task on novel and emerging entity recognition. In *Proceedings of the 3rd Workshop on Noisy User-generated Text, NUT@EMNLP 2017, Copenhagen, Denmark, September 7, 2017*, pages 140–147.

Cícero Nogueira Dos Santos and Bianca Zadrozny. 2014. Learning character-level representations for part-of-speech tagging. In *Proceedings of the 31st International Conference on International Conference on Machine Learning - Volume 32*, ICML'14, pages II–1818–II–1826. JMLR.org.

Matt Gardner, Joel Grus, Mark Neumann, Oyvind Tafjord, Pradeep Dasigi, Nelson F. Liu, Matthew Peters, Michael Schmitz, and Luke S. Zettlemoyer. 2017. Allennlp: A deep semantic natural language processing platform.

Kevin Gimpel, Nathan Schneider, Brendan O'Connor, Dipanjan Das, Daniel Mills, Jacob Eisenstein, Michael Heilman, Dani Yogatama, Jeffrey Flanigan, and Noah A. Smith. 2011. Part-of-speech tagging for twitter: Annotation, features, and experiments. In *The 49th Annual Meeting of the Association for Computational Linguistics: Human Language Technologies, Proceedings of the Conference, 19-24 June, 2011, Portland, Oregon, USA - Short Papers*, pages 42–47.

Rafal Józefowicz, Oriol Vinyals, Mike Schuster, Noam Shazeer, and Yonghui Wu. 2016. Exploring the limits of language modeling. *CoRR*, abs/1602.02410.

Nal Kalchbrenner, Edward Grefenstette, and Phil Blunsom. 2014. A convolutional neural network for modelling sentences. In *Proceedings of the 52nd Annual Meeting of the Association for Computational Linguistics (Volume 1: Long Papers)*, pages 655–665, Baltimore, Maryland. Association for Computational Linguistics.

Yoon Kim. 2014. Convolutional neural networks for sentence classification. In *Proceedings of the 2014 Conference on Empirical Methods in Natural Language Processing, EMNLP 2014, October 25-29, 2014, Doha, Qatar, A meeting of SIGDAT, a Special Interest Group of the ACL*, pages 1746–1751.

Yoon Kim, Yacine Jernite, David Sontag, and Alexander M. Rush. 2016. Character-aware neural language models. In *Proceedings of the Thirtieth AAAI Conference on Artificial Intelligence, February 12-17, 2016, Phoenix, Arizona, USA.*, pages 2741–2749.

Guillaume Lample, Miguel Ballesteros, Sandeep Subramanian, Kazuya Kawakami, and Chris Dyer. 2016. Neural architectures for named entity recognition. In *NAACL HLT 2016, The 2016 Conference of the North American Chapter of the Association for Computational Linguistics: Human Language Technologies, San Diego California, USA, June 12-17, 2016*, pages 260–270.

Wang Ling, Chris Dyer, Alan W. Black, Isabel Trancoso, Ramon Fermandez, Silvio Amir, Luís Marujo, and Tiago Luís. 2015. Finding function in form: Compositional character models for open vocabulary word representation. In *Proceedings of the 2015 Conference on Empirical Methods in Natural Language Processing, EMNLP 2015, Lisbon, Portugal, September 17-21, 2015*, pages 1520–1530.

Edward Loper and Steven Bird. 2002. Nltk: The natural language toolkit. In *Proceedings of the ACL-02 Workshop on Effective Tools and Methodologies for Teaching Natural Language Processing and Computational Linguistics - Volume 1*, ETMTNLP '02, pages 63–70, Stroudsburg, PA, USA. Association for Computational Linguistics.

Xuezhe Ma and Eduard Hovy. 2016. End-to-end sequence labeling via bi-directional lstm-cnns-crf. In *Proceedings of the 54th Annual Meeting of the Association for Computational Linguistics (Volume 1: Long Papers)*, pages 1064–1074, Berlin, Germany. Association for Computational Linguistics.

Christopher D. Manning, Mihai Surdeanu, John Bauer, Jenny Rose Finkel, Steven Bethard, and David McClosky. 2014. The stanford corenlp natural language processing toolkit. In *Proceedings of the 52nd Annual Meeting of the Association for Computational Linguistics, ACL 2014, June 22-27, 2014, Baltimore, MD, USA, System Demonstrations*, pages 55–60.

Gábor Melis, Chris Dyer, and Phil Blunsom. 2017. On the state of the art of evaluation in neural language models. *CoRR*, abs/1707.05589.

Graham Neubig, Chris Dyer, Yoav Goldberg, Austin Matthews, Waleed Ammar, Antonios Anastasopoulos, Miguel Ballesteros, David Chiang, Daniel Clothiaux, Trevor Cohn, Kevin Duh, Manaal Faruqui, Cynthia Gan, Dan Garrette, Yangfeng Ji, Lingpeng Kong, Adhiguna Kuncoro, Gaurav Kumar, Chaitanya Malaviya, Paul Michel, Yusuke Oda, Matthew Richardson, Naomi Saphra, Swabha Swayamdipta, and Pengcheng Yin. 2017a. Dynet: The dynamic neural network toolkit. *CoRR*, abs/1701.03980.

Graham Neubig, Chris Dyer, Yoav Goldberg, Austin Matthews, Waleed Ammar, Antonios Anastasopoulos, Miguel Ballesteros, David Chiang, Daniel Clothiaux, Trevor Cohn, Kevin Duh, Manaal

Faruqui, Cynthia Gan, Dan Garrette, Yangfeng Ji, Lingpeng Kong, Adhiguna Kuncoro, Gaurav Kumar, Chaitanya Malaviya, Paul Michel, Yusuke Oda, Matthew Richardson, Naomi Saphra, Swabha Swayamdipta, and Pengcheng Yin. 2017b. Dynet: The dynamic neural network toolkit. *CoRR*, abs/1701.03980.

Adam Paszke, Sam Gross, and Adam Lerer. 2017. Automatic differentiation in pytorch.

Matthew E. Peters, Waleed Ammar, Chandra Bhagavatula, and Russell Power. 2017. Semi-supervised sequence tagging with bidirectional language models. In *Proceedings of the 55th Annual Meeting of the Association for Computational Linguistics, ACL 2017, Vancouver, Canada, July 30 - August 4, Volume 1: Long Papers*, pages 1756–1765.

Matthew E Peters, Mark Neumann, Mohit Iyyer, Matt Gardner, Christopher Clark, Kenton Lee, and Luke Zettlemoyer. 2018. Deep contextualized word representations. *arXiv preprint arXiv:1802.05365*.

Nils Reimers and Iryna Gurevych. 2017. Reporting score distributions makes a difference: Performance study of lstm-networks for sequence tagging. In *Proceedings of the 2017 Conference on Empirical Methods in Natural Language Processing*, pages 338–348. Association for Computational Linguistics.

Erik F. Tjong Kim Sang and Fien De Meulder. 2003. Introduction to the conll-2003 shared task: Language-independent named entity recognition. In *Proceedings of the Seventh Conference on Natural Language Learning, CoNLL 2003, Held in cooperation with HLT-NAACL 2003, Edmonton, Canada, May 31 - June 1, 2003*, pages 142–147.

Richard Socher, A. V. Perelygin, Jean Wu, Jason Chuang, Christopher D. Manning, Andrew Ng, and Christopher Potts. 2013. Recursive deep models for semantic compositionality over a sentiment treebank. In *Conference on Empirical Methods in Natural Language Processing*.

Ellen M. Voorhees and Dawn M. Tice. 2000. Building a question answering test collection. In *SIGIR 2000: Proceedings of the 23rd Annual International ACM SIGIR Conference on Research and Development in Information Retrieval, July 24-28, 2000, Athens, Greece*, pages 200–207.

Zhilin Yang, Zihang Dai, Ruslan Salakhutdinov, and William W. Cohen. 2017. Breaking the softmax bottleneck: A high-rank RNN language model. *CoRR*, abs/1711.03953.

Wojciech Zaremba, Ilya Sutskever, and Oriol Vinyals. 2014. Recurrent neural network regularization. *CoRR*, abs/1409.2329.

OpenSeq2Seq: Extensible Toolkit for Distributed and Mixed Precision Training of Sequence-to-Sequence Models

Oleksii Kuchaiev, Boris Ginsburg, Igor Gitman,
Vitaly Lavrukhin, Carl Case, Paulius Micikevicius
NVIDIA
Santa Clara, CA
{okuchaiev,bginsburg,igitman}@nvidia.com
{vlavrukhin,carlc,pauliusm}@nvidia.com

Abstract

We present OpenSeq2Seq – an open-source toolkit for training sequence-to-sequence models. The main goal of our toolkit is to allow researchers to most effectively explore different sequence-to-sequence architectures. The efficiency is achieved by fully supporting distributed and mixed-precision training.

OpenSeq2Seq provides building blocks for training encoder-decoder models for neural machine translation and automatic speech recognition. We plan to extend it with other modalities in the future.

1 Introduction

Sequence-to-Sequence models built around the encoder-decoder paradigm (Sutskever et al., 2014) have been successfully used for natural language processing (NLP) (Vaswani et al., 2017), image-captioning (Xu et al., 2015), and automatic speech recognition (ASR) (Chan et al., 2015; Battenberg et al., 2017). However, implementing a sequence-to-sequence model in a general purpose deep learning framework such as TensorFlow (Abadi et al., 2016), CNTK (Yu et al., 2014) or PyTorch (Paszke et al., 2017) can be challenging, especially with support for distributed training. Several open-source toolkits have been proposed in recent years in an attempt to tackle this challenge. Among the most popular ones are: OpenNMT (Klein et al., 2017), Seq2Seq (Britz et al., 2017), NMT (Luong et al., 2017), and Tensor2Tensor (Vaswani et al., 2017). These toolkits make it much easier to reproduce most current state-of-the-art results and train your own models on new datasets. OpenSeq2Seq is inspired by these approaches with an additional focus on distributed and mixed-precision training.

In particular, OpenSeq2Seq adds support for mixed precision training as described in (Micikevicius et al., 2017). It uses the IEEE float16 data format to reduce memory requirements and speed up training on modern deep learning hardware such as NVIDIA's Volta GPUs. Furthermore, OpenSeq2Seq supports multi-GPU and multi-node distributed training.

OpenSeq2Seq is built using TensorFlow and is available at: `https://github.com/NVIDIA/OpenSeq2Seq`.

2 Design

The main design goals of OpenSeq2Seq are extensibility and modularity. It provides several core abstract classes which users can inherit from when adding new models: `DataLayer`, `Model`, `Encoder`, `Decoder` and `Loss`. The `Model` class implements distributed and mixed precision training support. For distributed training we support two modes, both following data-parallel approaches with synchronous updates: (1) multi-tower mode in which a separate TensorFlow graph is built on every GPU and (2) Horovod-based mode (Sergeev and Del Balso, 2018) which allows both *multi-node* as well as *multi-GPU* executions.

At a high level, the `Encoder` is a model block which consumes data and produces a representation; while the `Decoder` is a model block which consumes a representation and produces data and/or output. While we do not strictly enforce this, we assume that any encoder can be combined with any decoder, thus improving flexibility and simplicity of experimentation. Note that it is possible to have a model consisting of only an encoder, only a decoder, or having more than one encoder and/or decoder. Currently, we provide the DataLayer, Encoder, Decoder and Loss class implementations for neural machine trans-

Proceedings of Workshop for NLP Open Source Software, pages 41–46
Melbourne, Australia, July 20, 2018. ©2018 Association for Computational Linguistics

lation (NMT) and automatic speech recognition (ASR) tasks.

2.1 API

OpenSeq2Seq provides a top-level `run.py` script which takes a flexible Python configuration file specifying the model and execution mode (*train*, *eval*, *train_eval* or *infer*). The configuration file allows user to specify parts of the model (i.e. data layer, encoder, decoder and loss) and their configuration parameters. Since the configuration file is written in Python, it is possible to provide actual Python classes as parameters. This maximizes flexibility by enabling users to define their own implementations for various components (e.g. encoders-decoders or even a custom learning rate decay schedules) without modifying the toolkit source code.

3 Mixed Precision support

OpenSeq2Seq fully supports training with mixed precision using float16 data types to utilize the newest GPUs. When using float16 to train large state-of-the art models, it is sometimes necessary to apply certain algorithmic techniques and keep some outputs in float32 (hence, mixed precision) to achieve best results. For mixed precision training we follow an algorithmic recipe from (Micikevicius et al., 2017). At a high level it can be summarized as follows:

1. Maintain float32 master copy of weights for weights update while using the float16 weights for forward and back propagation

2. Apply loss scaling while computing gradients to prevent underflow during backpropagation

It is worth mentioning that both (1)-(2) are not always necessary. However, this method has proven to be robust across a variety of large set of complex models (Micikevicius et al., 2017).

Note that while having two copies of weights increase the memory consumption for weights, the total memory requirements for mixed precision is often *decreased* because activations, activation gradients, and other intermediate tensors can now be kept in float16. This is especially beneficial for models with a high degree of parameter sharing, such as recurrent models.

3.1 Mixed Precision Optimizer

Our implementation is different from the previous approach[1]: instead of a custom variable getter, we introduce a wrapper around standard TensorFlow optimizers. The model is created with float16 data type, so all variables and gradients are in float16 by default (except for the layers which are explicitly redefined as float32; for example data layers or operations on CPU). The wrapper then automatically converts float16 gradients to float32 and submits them to TensorFlow's optimizer, which updates the master copy of weights in float32. Updated float32 weights are converted back to float16 weigths, which are used by the model in the next forward-backward iteration. Figure 1 illustrates the `MixedPrecisionOptimizerWrapper` architecture.

3.2 Mixed Precision Regularizer

Training in mixed precision may need special care for regularization. Consider, for example, weight decay regularization when weights decay term $2\lambda * w$ is added to the gradients with respect to the loss $\frac{\partial L}{\partial w}$. Given that the weights are commonly initialized with small values, multiplying them with weight decay coefficient λ which is usually on the order of $[10^{-5}, 10^{-3}]$ can result in numerical underflow.

To overcome this problem we use the following approach. First, all regularizers should be defined during variable creation (a regularizer parameter in the `tf.get_variable` function or `tf.layers` objects). Second, the regularizer function should be wrapped with `mp_regularizer_wrapper` function which does two things. First, it adds variable with the user-provided regularization function to the TensorFlow collection. Second, it disables the underlying regularization function for float16 copy. The created collection will later be retrieved by `MixedPrecisionOptimizerWrapper` and the corresponding functions will be applied to the float32 copy of the weights ensuring that their gradients always stay in full precision. Since this regularization is not in the loss computation graph, we explicitly call `tf.gradients` and add the result to the gradients passed in the `compute_gradients` in the optimizer.

[1] `http://docs.nvidia.com/deeplearning/sdk/mixed-precision-training/`. Accessed: 2018-04-06.

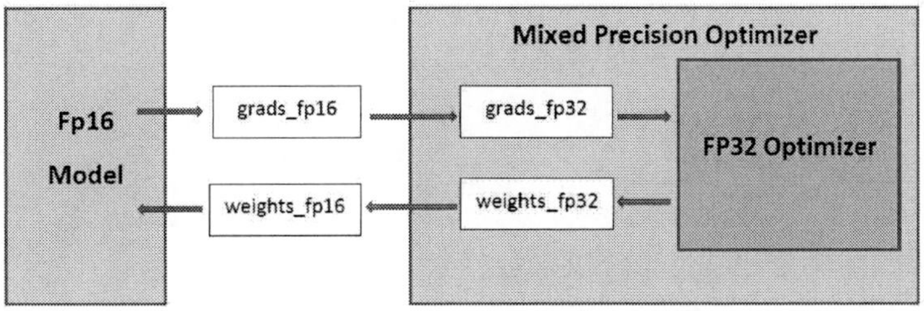

Figure 1: "Mixed precision" optimizer wrapper around any TensorFlow optimizer

3.3 Automatic Loss Scaling

The mixed precision training approach suggests that the user set a fixed *loss scale* hyper-parameter to adjust the dynamic range of backpropagation to match the dynamic range of float16 (Micikevicius et al., 2017). OpenSeq2Seq implements an *automatic loss scaling* so the user does not have to select the loss-scale value manually. The optimizer inspects the parameter gradients at each iteration and uses their values to select the loss scale for the *next* iteration.

Model	Iteration	Score
GNMT-like float32	340K	23.21 BLEU
GNMT-like mixed	340K	23.63 BLEU
Transformer float32	220K	25.2 BLEU
Transformer mixed	220K	25.4 BLEU
DS2-like float32	110K	4.59% WER
DS2-like mixed	110K	4.47% WER

Table 1: Evaluation scores after training using float32 and mixed precision. We used 2, 4 and 8 GPUs to train Transformer, GNMT and DeepSpeech2 models. All configs are available on OpenSeq2Seq's GitHub.

4 Machine Translation and Automatic Speech Recognition

NMT and ASE are two modalities which currently have full implementation in OpenSeq2Seq.

4.1 NMT experiments

Neural Machine Translation (NMT) is naturally expressed in terms of encoder-decoder paradigm (Bahdanau et al., 2014; Wu et al., 2016; Vaswani et al., 2017). OpenSeq2Seq provides several encoder and decoder implementations for this task - RNN and non-RNN based ones with various types of attention. It has all the necessary blocks for GNMT-like (Wu et al., 2016) and Transformer (Vaswani et al., 2017) models. Also, these blocks can be easily mixed together.

For example, if the user wants to train GNMT-like (Wu et al., 2016) model he/she needs to construct a configuration file which uses `GNMTLikeEncoderWithEmbedding` as the encoder, and `RNNDecoderWithAttention` as the decoder for training and `BeamSearchRNNDecoderWithAttention` for inference. The precision mode (float32, float16 or mixed) as well as the number of GPUs and other parameters are also specified in the configuration file.

For training using mixed precision we do not change network topology or any of the hyper parameters. Figure 2 (A) demonstrates that training loss curves for GNMT-like model using float32 and mixed precision track each other very closely during training (the same is true for Transformer training). In our experiments, we used WMT 2016 English→German data set obtained by combining the Europarlv7, News Commentary v10, and Common Crawl corpora and resulting in roughly 4.5 million sentence pairs. Table 1 compares BLEU scores after training with float32 and mixed precision. These scores are computed using *multi-bleu.perl*[2] script from Moses against *newstest2013.tok.de* file.

In our experiments, for Transformer and GNMT-like model, total GPU memory consumption is reduced to about 55% of what it was while using float32. We also observe performance boosts (around x1.8 for GNMT) which can vary depending on the batch size. The general rule of thumb is that bigger batch size yields better performance.

[2] `https://github.com/moses-smt/mosesdecoder/blob/master/scripts/generic/multi-bleu.perl`

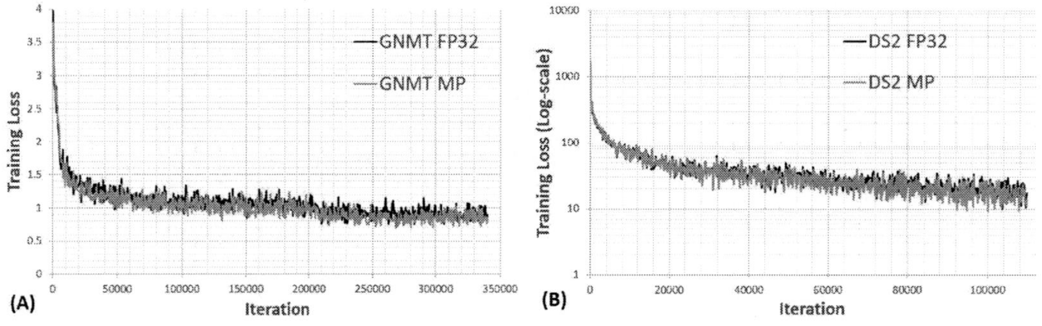

Figure 2: Training loss curves for: (A) GNMT-like model, and (B) DeepSpeech2-like model using float32 and mixed precision. For both models, float32 and mixed precision training very closely match each other.

4.2 ASR experiments

Many recent Automated Speech Recognition (ASR) models are built using explicit encoder-decoder topology (Battenberg et al., 2017; Prabhavalkar et al., 2017; Chiu et al., 2017). However, even for models without explicit encoder-decoder topology, it is easy to re-formulate them as such in our toolkit. For example, let's consider an encoder-decoder implementation of Deep Speech 2 (DS2) model (Amodei et al., 2016) in OpenSeq2Seq. DS2 consists of three convolutional layers, several bidirectional or unidirectional recurrent layers (with LSTMs or GRUs), an optional row convolutional layer, and a fully connected layer followed by a hidden layer which produces logits for the Connectionist Temporal Classification (CTC) loss (Graves et al., 2006). Logits represent a probability distribution over alphabet characters at each timestep. A beam search CTC decoder with language model re-scorer is usually employed for producing the output characters sequence during inference. While DS2 doesn't contain explicit encoder and decoder (in seq2seq sense), we can split the model in the following fashion: convolutional, recurrent and fully connected layers are encapsulated in the `DeepSpeech2Encoder`, and logits' hidden layer together with the CTC decoder are encapsulated in the `FullyConnectedCTCDecoder`. The reason behind this split point is simple: it allows the encoder to output a custom-sized representation and it encourages encoder and decoder re-use. For example, the CTC decoder can be replaced with any decoder from text-to-text models.

In our experiments, we trained DeepSpeech2-like model on a "clean" and "other" subsets of LibriSpeech training dataset (Panayotov et al., 2015). Table 1 shows final Word Error Rates (WER)[3] on LibriSpeech "dev-clean" subset, obtained after training using float32 and mixed precision. Similarly to GNMT experiments, we did not change any of the hyper parameters when training in mixed precision. During training in mixed precision, we observed a total memory reduction to around 57% compared to float32 mode. Figure 2 (B) demonstrates that mixed precision has no effect on convergence behaviour.

5 Conclusion and future plans

Modern deep learning hardware is moving towards training with low precision. NVIDIA's Volta-based GPUs offer significant performance boost and reduced memory footprint while training using Tensor Cores (e.g. using float16)[4]. OpenSeq2Seq natively supports training using mixed precision and allows NLP and ASR researchers to increase their productivity. In our experiments, we see total memory reductions to 55%–57% of float32 mode for GNMT, Transformer and DeepSpeech2 models.

OpenSeq2Seq aims to offer a rich library of commonly used encoders and decoders. We plan to extend it with other modalities such as text-to-speech and image-to-text. Finally, we are working on providing more encoder and decoder choices for already supported tasks such as machine translation and speech recognition.

[3] With beam width = 2048 and language model provided by Mozilla: `https://github.com/mozilla/DeepSpeech/tree/master/data/lm`

[4] `http://images.nvidia.com/content/volta-architecture/pdf/volta-architecture-whitepaper.pdf`

Acknowledgments

We are grateful to Siddharth Bhatnagar and Luyang Chen for their work on previous version of the toolkit. We would like to thank Hao Wu, Ben Barsdell, Nathan Luehr, Jonah Alben, and Ujval Kapasi for their fruitful discussions.

References

Martín Abadi, Paul Barham, Jianmin Chen, Zhifeng Chen, Andy Davis, Jeffrey Dean, Matthieu Devin, Sanjay Ghemawat, Geoffrey Irving, Michael Isard, et al. 2016. Tensorflow: A system for large-scale machine learning. In *OSDI*, volume 16, pages 265–283.

Dario Amodei, Rishita Anubhai, Eric Battenberg, Carl Case, Jared Casper, Bryan Catanzaro, Jingdong Chen, Mike Chrzanowski, Adam Coates, Greg Diamos, Erich Elsen, Jesse Engel, Linxi Fan, Christopher Fougner, Awni Y. Hannun, Billy Jun, Tony Han, Patrick LeGresley, Xiangang Li, Libby Lin, Sharan Narang, Andrew Y. Ng, Sherjil Ozair, Ryan Prenger, Sheng Qian, Jonathan Raiman, Sanjeev Satheesh, David Seetapun, Shubho Sengupta, Chong Wang, Yi Wang, Zhiqian Wang, Bo Xiao, Yan Xie, Dani Yogatama, Jun Zhan, and Zhenyao Zhu. 2016. Deep speech 2 : End-to-end speech recognition in english and mandarin. In *ICML*.

Dzmitry Bahdanau, Kyunghyun Cho, and Yoshua Bengio. 2014. Neural machine translation by jointly learning to align and translate. *arXiv preprint arXiv:1409.0473*.

Eric Battenberg, Jitong Chen, Rewon Child, Adam Coates, Yashesh Gaur, Yi Li, Hairong Liu, Sanjeev Satheesh, David Seetapun, Anuroop Sriram, et al. 2017. Exploring neural transducers for end-to-end speech recognition. *arXiv preprint arXiv:1707.07413*.

Denny Britz, Anna Goldie, Thang Luong, and Quoc Le. 2017. Massive Exploration of Neural Machine Translation Architectures. *ArXiv e-prints*.

William Chan, Navdeep Jaitly, Quoc V Le, and Oriol Vinyals. 2015. Listen, attend and spell.

Chung-Cheng Chiu, Tara N Sainath, Yonghui Wu, Rohit Prabhavalkar, Patrick Nguyen, Zhifeng Chen, Anjuli Kannan, Ron J Weiss, Kanishka Rao, Katya Gonina, et al. 2017. State-of-the-art speech recognition with sequence-to-sequence models. *arXiv preprint arXiv:1712.01769*.

Alex Graves, Santiago Fernández, Faustino Gomez, and Jürgen Schmidhuber. 2006. Connectionist temporal classification: labelling unsegmented sequence data with recurrent neural networks. In *Proceedings of the 23rd international conference on Machine learning*, pages 369–376. ACM.

Guillaume Klein, Yoon Kim, Yuntian Deng, Jean Senellart, and Alexander M. Rush. 2017. Opennmt: Open-source toolkit for neural machine translation. In *Proc. ACL*.

Minh-Thang Luong, Eugene Brevdo, and Rui Zhao. 2017. Neural machine translation (seq2seq) tutorial. *https://github.com/tensorflow/nmt*.

Paulius Micikevicius, Sharan Narang, Jonah Alben, Gregory Diamos, Erich Elsen, David Garcia, Boris Ginsburg, Michael Houston, Oleksii Kuchaev, Ganesh Venkatesh, et al. 2017. Mixed precision training. *arXiv preprint arXiv:1710.03740*.

Vassil Panayotov, Guoguo Chen, Daniel Povey, and Sanjeev Khudanpur. 2015. Librispeech: an asr corpus based on public domain audio books. In *Acoustics, Speech and Signal Processing (ICASSP), 2015 IEEE International Conference on*, pages 5206–5210. IEEE.

Adam Paszke, Sam Gross, Soumith Chintala, Gregory Chanan, Edward Yang, Zachary DeVito, Zeming Lin, Alban Desmaison, Luca Antiga, and Adam Lerer. 2017. Automatic differentiation in pytorch.

Rohit Prabhavalkar, Kanishka Rao, Tara N Sainath, Bo Li, Leif Johnson, and Navdeep Jaitly. 2017. A comparison of sequence-to-sequence models for speech recognition. In *Proc. Interspeech*, pages 939–943.

Alexander Sergeev and Mike Del Balso. 2018. Horovod: fast and easy distributed deep learning in tensorflow. *arXiv preprint arXiv:1802.05799*.

Ilya Sutskever, Oriol Vinyals, and Quoc V Le. 2014. Sequence to sequence learning with neural networks. In Z. Ghahramani, M. Welling, C. Cortes, N. D. Lawrence, and K. Q. Weinberger, editors, *Advances in Neural Information Processing Systems 27*, pages 3104–3112. Curran Associates, Inc.

Ashish Vaswani, Noam Shazeer, Niki Parmar, Jakob Uszkoreit, Llion Jones, Aidan N Gomez, Łukasz Kaiser, and Illia Polosukhin. 2017. Attention is all you need. In *Advances in Neural Information Processing Systems*, pages 6000–6010.

Yonghui Wu, Mike Schuster, Zhifeng Chen, Quoc V Le, Mohammad Norouzi, Wolfgang Macherey, Maxim Krikun, Yuan Cao, Qin Gao, Klaus Macherey, et al. 2016. Google's neural machine translation system: Bridging the gap between human and machine translation. *arXiv preprint arXiv:1609.08144*.

Kelvin Xu, Jimmy Ba, Ryan Kiros, Kyunghyun Cho, Aaron Courville, Ruslan Salakhudinov, Rich Zemel, and Yoshua Bengio. 2015. Show, attend and tell: Neural image caption generation with visual attention. In *International Conference on Machine Learning*, pages 2048–2057.

Dong Yu, Adam Eversole, Mike Seltzer, Kaisheng Yao, Zhiheng Huang, Brian Guenter, Oleksii Kuchaiev, Yu Zhang, Frank Seide, Huaming Wang, et al. 2014. An introduction to computational networks and the computational network toolkit. *Microsoft Technical Report MSR-TR-2014–112*.

SUMMA: Integrating Multiple NLP Technologies into an Open-source Platform for Multilingual Media Monitoring

Ulrich Germann
University of Edinburgh
ugermann@ed.ac.uk

Renārs Liepiņš
LETA
renars.liepins@leta.lv

Didzis Gosko
LETA
didzis.gosko@leta.lv

Guntis Barzdins
University of Latvia
guntis.barzdins@lu.lv

Abstract

The open-source SUMMA Platform is a highly scalable distributed architecture for monitoring a large number of media broadcasts in parallel, with a lag behind actual broadcast time of at most a few minutes.

It assembles numerous state-of-the-art NLP technologies into a fully automated media ingestion pipeline that can record live broadcasts, detect and transcribe spoken content, translate from several languages (original text or transcribed speech) into English,[1] recognize Named Entities, detect topics, cluster and summarize documents across language barriers, and extract and store factual claims in these news items.

This paper describes the intended use cases and discusses the system design decisions that allowed us to integrate state-of-the-art NLP modules into an effective workflow with comparatively little effort.

1 Introduction

SUMMA ("Scalable Understanding of Multilingual Media") is an EU-funded collaborative effort to combine state-of-the-art NLP components into a functioning, scalable media content processing pipeline to support large news organizations in their daily work. The project consortium comprises seven acadamic / research partners — the University of Edinburgh, the Lativan Information Agency (LETA), Idiap Research Institute, Priberam Labs, Qatar Computing Research Institute, University College London, and Sheffield University —, and BBC Monitoring and Deutsche Welle as use case partners.

In this paper, we first describe the use cases that the platform addresses, and then the design decisions that allowed us to integrate existing state-of-the art NLP technologies into a highly scalable, coherent platform with comparatively little integration effort.

2 Use Cases

Three use cases drive the development of the SUMMA Platform.

2.1 External Media Monitoring

BBC Monitoring is a business unit within the British Broadcasting Corporation (BBC). In continuous operation since 1939, it provides media monitoring, analysis, and translations of foreign news content to the BBC's news rooms, the British Government, and other subscribers to its services. Each of its ca. 300 monitoring journalists usually keeps track up to 4 live sources in parallel (typically TV channels received via satellite), plus a number of other sources of information such as social media feeds. Assuming work distributed around the clock in three shifts,[2] BBC Monitoring thus currently has, on average, the capacity to actively monitor about 400 live broadcasts at any given time — just over a quarter of the ca. 1,500 TV stations that it has access to, not to mention other sources such as radio broadcasts and streams on the internet. NLP technologies such as automatic speech recognition (ASR), machine translation (MT), and named entity (NE) tagging can alleviate the human media monitors from mundane monitoring tasks and let them focus on media digestion and analysis.

2.2 Internal Monitoring

Deutsche Welle is an international broadcaster operating world-wide in 30 different languages. Regional news rooms produce and broadcast content independently; journalistic and programming decisions are **not** made by a central authority within Deutsche Welle. Therefore, it is difficult for the overall organisation to maintain an accurate and up-to-date overview of what is being broadcast, and what stories have been covered.

[1] The choice of English as the lingua franca within the Platform is due to the working language of our use case partners; the highly modular design of the Platform allows the easy integration of custom translation engines, if required.

[2] The actual distribution of staff allocation over the course of the day may differ.

Proceedings of Workshop for NLP Open Source Software, pages 47–51
Melbourne, Australia, July 20, 2018.

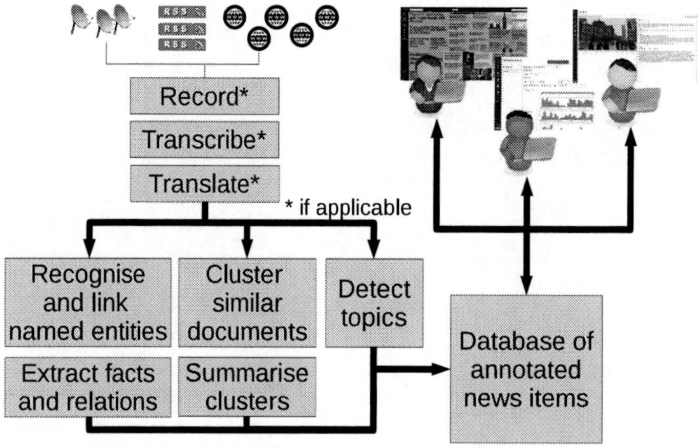

Figure 1: The SUMMA Platform Workflow

The Platform's cross-lingual story clustering and summarization module with the corresponding online visualization tool addresses this need. It provides an aggregate view of recent captured broadcasts, with easy access to individual broadcast segments in each cluster.

2.3 Data Journalism

The third use case is the use of the Platform's database of news coverage for investigations involving large amounts of news reports, for example, exploring how certain persons or issues are portrayed in the media over time.

3 System Overview

Figure 1 shows the overall system architecture. The SUMMA Platform consists of three major parts: a data ingestion pipeline built mostly upon existing state-of-the-art NLP technology; a web-based user front-end specifically developed with the intended use cases in mind; and a database at the center that is continuously updated by the data ingestion pipeline and accessed by end users through the web-based GUI, or through a REST API by downstream applications.

The user interfaces and the database structure were custom developments for the SUMMA Platform. The grapical user interfaces are based on input from potential users and wireframe designs provided by the use case partners. They are implemented in the Aurelia JavaScript Client Framework[3]. For NLP processing, we mostly build on and integrate existing NLP technology. We describe key components below.

3.1 Languages Covered

The goal of the project to offer NLP capabilities for English, German, Arabic, Russian, Spanish, Latvian, Farsi, Portuguese, and Ukrainian. We currently cover the former 6; the latter 3 are work in progress.

Due to the large number of individual components (number of languages covered times NLP technologies), it is not possible to go into details about training data used and individual component performance here. Such details are covered in the SUMMA project deliverables D3.1 (Garner et al., 2017), D4.1 (Obamuyide et al., 2017), and D5.1 (Mendes et al., 2017), which are available from the project's web site.[4] We include applicable deliverable numbers in parentheses below, so that the inclined reader can follow up on details.

3.2 Live Stream Recorder and Chunker

The recorder and chunker monitors one or more live streams via their respective URLs. Broadcast signals received via satellite are converted into transport streams suitable for streaming via the internet and provided via a web interface. This happens outside of the platform since it requires special hardware. The access point is a live stream provided as an `.m3u8` playlist via a web interface that is polled regularly by the respective data feed module.

All data received by the Recorder-and-Chunker is recorded to disk und chunked into 5-minutes segments for further processing. Within the Platform infrastructure, the Recorder-and-Chunker also serves as the internal video server for recorded

[3] `aurelia.io`

[4] `www.summa-project.eu/deliverables`

transitory material, i.e., material not obtained from persistent sources.

Once downloaded and chunked, a document stub with the internal video URL is entered into the data base, which then notifies the task scheduler about the new arrival, which in turn schedules the item for downstream processing.

Video and audio files that are not transitory but provided by the original sources in more persistent forms (i.e., served from a permanent location), are currently not recorded[5] but retrieved from the original source when needed.

3.3 Other Data Feeds

Text-based data is retrieved by data feed modules that poll the providing source at regular intervals for new data. The data is downloaded and entered into the database, which then again notifies the task scheduler, which in turn schedules the new arrivals for downstream processing.

In addition to a generic RSS feed monitor, we use custom data monitors that are tailored to specific data sources, e.g. the specific APIs that broadcaster-specific news apps use for updates. The main task of these specialized modules is to map between data fields of the source API's specific response (typically in JSON[6] format), and the data fields used within the Platform.

3.4 Automatic Speech Recognition (D3.1)

The ASR modules within the Platform are built on top of CloudASR (Klejch et al., 2015); the underlying speech recognition models are trained with the Kaldi toolkit (Povey et al., 2011). Punctuation is added using a neural MT engine that was trained to translate from un-punctuated text to punctuation. The training data for the punctuation module is created by stripping punctuation from an existing corpus of news texts. The MT engine used for punctuation insertion uses the same software components as the MT engines used for language translation.

3.5 Machine Translation (D3.1)

The machine translation engines for language translation currently use the Marian[7] decoder (Junczys-Dowmunt et al., 2016) for translation with neural MT models trained with the Nematus toolkit (Sennrich et al., 2017). We have recently switched to the Marian toolkit for training.

3.6 Topic Classification (D3.1)

The topic classifier uses a hierarchical attention model for document classification (Yang et al., 2016) trained on nearly 600K manually annotated documents in 8 languages.

3.7 Storyline Clustering (D3.1) and Cluster Summarization (D5.1)

Incoming stories are clustered into storylines with Aggarwal and Yu's (2006) online clustering algorithm. The resulting storylines are summarized with the extractive summarization algorithm by Almeida and Martins (2013).

3.8 Named Entity Recognition and Linking (D4.1)

For Named Entity Recognition, we use TurboEntityRecognizer, a component within TurboParser[8] (Martins et al., 2009). Recognized entities and relations between them (or propositions about them) about them are linked to a knowledge base of facts using techniques developed by Paikens et al. (2016).

3.9 Databases

The Platform currently relies on two databases. The central database in the NLP processing pipeline is an instance of RethinkDB[9], a document-oriented database that allows clients to subscribe to a continuous stream of notifications about changes in the database. This allows clients (e.g. the task scheduler) to be notified about the lastest incoming items as they are added to the database, without the need to poll the database periodically. Each document consists of several fields, such as the URL of the original news item, a transcript for audio sources, or the original text, a translation into English if applicable, entities such as persons, organisations or locations mentioned in the news items, etc.

For interaction with web-based user interfaces, we are using a PostgreSQL[10] database, which is periodically updated with the latest arrivals from the data ingestion pipeline. This second database was not part of the original design; it was added out of performance concerns, as we noticed at some point that RethinkDB's responsiveness tended to deteriorate over time as the number of items in the database grew. Ultimately, this turned out to be an error in the set-up of our RethinkDB instance: certain crucial fields weren't indexed, so that RethinkDB resorted to a linear search for certain operations. The current split between two databases is not ideal; however, it is operational and eliminating it is not a high priority on the current development agenda.

[5] On a marginal note, recording a single live stream produces, depending on video resolution, up to 25 GiB of data per day.

[6] `https://www.json.org`

[7] `www.github.com/marian-nmt`

[8] `https://github.com/andre-martins/TurboParser`

[9] `www.rethinkdb.com`

[10] `www.postgresql.org`

4 Platform Design and Implementation

As is obvious from the description above, the Platform utilizes numerous existing technologies. In designing and implementing the Platform, we had two main objectives:

1. Minimize the effort necessary to integrate the various existing technologies.
2. Keep individual NLP components as independent as possible, so that they can be re-used for other purposes as well.

In order to meet these objectives, we designed the processing pipeline as a federation of microservices that communicate with each other via REST APIs and/or a message queue.

For rapid prototyping, we defined REST APIs for each NLP module within the OpenAPI Specification Framework[11]. The suite of Swagger tools[12] associated with OpenAPI allowed us to specify REST APIs quickly and generate boilerplate code for the back-end server of each microservice. This reduced integration efforts to implementing a few back-end functions for each RESTful server — in whatever programming language the contributing partner felt most comfortable with.

In the Platform prototype, we used separate processes that act as dedicated intermediaries between the message queue[13] and each individual NLP component. As the Platform matures, we gradually moving to implementing RabbitMQ interfaces directly with the NLP processors, to eliminate the intermediaries and reduce the overall complexity of the system.

One of the great advantages of using a message queue is that it makes scaling and load balancing easy. If we need more throughput, we add more workers (possibly on different machines) that talk to the same message queues. Each type of task has two queues: one for open requests, the other one for completed requests. Each worker loops over waiting for a message to appear in the queue, popping it of it, acknowledging it upon successful completion (so that it can be marked as done), and pushing the response onto the respective queue. Workers need not be aware of the overall architecture of the system; only the overall task scheduler has to be aware of the actual work flow.

Maintaining the RESTful APIs is nevertheless worthwhile: it allows individual components to be deployed easily as a service outside of the Platform's context and workflow.

The overall NLP processing workflow is designed as an icremental annotation process: each service augments incoming media items with additional information: automatic speech recognition (ASR) services add transcriptions, machine translation (MT) engines add translations, and so forth.

Each component of the Platform runs independently in a Docker[14] application container. Similar to conventional virtual machines (VMs), Docker containers isolate applications from the host system by running them in a separate environment ("container"), so that each application can use its own set of libraries, ports, etc. However, unlike conventional VMs, which emulate a complete machine including device and memory management, the Docker engine allows containers to share the host's kernel and resources, greatly reducing the virtualisation / containerization overhead. For small-scale single-host deployment (up to ten live streams on a 32-core server), we use Docker Compose;[15] for multi-host scaling, Docker Swarm[16].

Another great advantage of the Docker platform is that many third-party components that we rely on (message queue, data bases) are available as pre-compiled Docker containers, so that their deployment within the Platform is trivial. No dependencies to manage, no compilation from scratch required, no conflicts with the OS on the host machine.

Our approach to the design of the Platform has several advantages over tigher integration within a single development framework in which contributing partners would be required to provide software libraries for one or more specific programming languages.

First, in line with our first design objective, it minimizes the integration overhead.

Second, it is agnostic to implementational choices and software dependencies of individual components. Each contributing partner can continue to work within their preferred development environment.[17]

Third, it provides for easy scalability of the system, as the Platform can be easily distributed over multiple hosts. With the message queue approach, multiple workers providing identical services can share the processing load.

Fourth, modules can be updated without having to re-build the entire system. Even live continuous upgrades and server migration can be accomplished easily by starting up a new instance of a specific service and then shutting down the obso-

[11] `www.openapis.org`; formerly Swagger

[12] `www.swagger.io`

[13] RabbitMQ (`https://www.rabbitmq.com/`) works well for us.

[14] `www.docker.com`

[15] `https://docs.docker.com/compose/`

[16] `https://docs.docker.com/engine/swarm`

[17] In the case of Windows-based software, however, licensing issues have to be considered for deployment in container environments such as Docker.

lete one.

Fifth, meeting our second design objective, the strong modularization of the Platform allows for easy re-use of components. The back-end server for each component can easily be integrated into other applications (albeit potentially requiring augmentations to the API).

5 Conclusion

We have reported on our experiences in implementing a high-performance, highly scalable natural language processing pipeline from existing implementations of state-of-the art as an assembly of containerized micro-services. We found that this approach greatly facilitated technology integration and collaboration, as it eliminated many points of potential friction, such as having to agree on a joint software development framework, adapting libraries, and dealing with software dependencies. Using the Docker platform, we are able to deploy and scale the Platform quickly.

Availability

The Platform infrastructure and most of its components are scheduled to be released as open-source software by the end of August 2018 and will be available through the project web site at

`www.summa-project.eu`.

Acknowledgements

This work was conducted within the scope of the Research and Innovation Action *SUMMA*, which has received funding from the European Union's Horizon 2020 research and innovation programme under grant agreement No 688139.

References

Aggarwal, Charu C and Philip S Yu. 2006. "A framework for clustering massive text and categorical data streams." *SIAM Int'l. Conf. on Data Mining*, 479–483.

Almeida, Miguel B and Andre FT Martins. 2013. "Fast and robust compressive summarization with dual decomposition and multi-task learning." *ACL*, 196–206.

Garner, Philip N., Alexandra Birch, Andrei Popescu-Belis, Peter Bell, Herve Bourlard, Steve Renals, Sebastião Miranda, and Ulrich Germann. 2017. *SUMMA Deliverable D3.1: Initial Progress Report on Shallow Stream Processing.* Tech. rep., The SUMMA Consortium.

Junczys-Dowmunt, Marcin, Tomasz Dwojak, and Hieu Hoang. 2016. "Is neural machine translation ready for deployment? A case study on 30 translation directions." *International Workshop on Spoken Language Translation.* Seattle, WA, USA.

Klejch, Ondřej, Ondřej Plátek, Lukáš Žilka, and Filip Jurčíček. 2015. "CloudASR: platform and service." *Int'l. Conf. on Text, Speech, and Dialogue*, 334–341.

Martins, André FT, Noah A Smith, and Eric P Xing. 2009. "Concise integer linear programming formulations for dependency parsing." *ACL*, 342–350.

Mendes, Afonso, Pedro Balage, Mariana Almeida, Sebastião Miranda, Nikos Papasarantopoulos, Shashi Narayan, and Shay Cohen. 2017. *SUMMA Deliverable 5.1: Initial Progress Report on Natural Language Understanding.* Tech. rep., The SUMMA Consortium.

Obamuyide, Abiola, Andreas Vlachos, Jeff Mitchell, David Nogueira, Sebastian Riedel, Filipe Aleixo, Samuel Broscheit, Andre Martins, Mariana Almeida, Sebastião Miranda, Afonso Mendes, and Andrei Popescu-Belis. 2017. *SUMMA Deliverable D4.1: Initial Progress Report on Automatic Knowledge Base Creation.* Tech. rep., The SUMMA Consortium.

Paikens, Peteris, Guntis Barzdins, Afonso Mendes, Daniel Ferreira, Samuel Broscheit, Mariana S. C. Almeida, Sebastião Miranda, David Nogueira, Pedro Balage, and André F. T. Martins. 2016. "SUMMA at TAC knowledge base population task 2016." *TAC.* Gaithersburg, Maryland, USA.

Povey, Daniel, Arnab Ghoshal, Gilles Boulianne, Lukáš Burget, Ondřej Glembek, Nagendra Goel, Mirko Hannemann, Petr Motlíček, Yanmin Qian, Petr Schwarz, Jan Silovský, Georg Stemmer, and Karel Veselý. 2011. "The Kaldi speech recognition toolkit." *ASRU.*

Sennrich, Rico, Orhan Firat, Kyunghyun Cho, Alexandra Birch, Barry Haddow, Julian Hitschler, Marcin Junczys-Dowmunt, Samuel Läubli, Antonio Valerio Miceli Barone, Jozef Mokry, and Maria Nadejde. 2017. "Nematus: a toolkit for neural machine translation." *EACL Demonstration Session.* Valencia, Spain.

Yang, Zichao, Diyi Yang, Chris Dyer, Xiaodong He, Alexander J. Smola, and Eduard H. Hovy. 2016. "Hierarchical attention networks for document classification." *NAACL.* San Diego, CA, USA.

The Annotated Transformer

Alexander M. Rush
srush@seas.harvard.edu
Harvard University

Abstract

A major aim of open-source NLP is to quickly and accurately reproduce the results of new work, in a manner that the community can easily use and modify. While most papers publish enough detail for replication, it still may be difficult to achieve good results in practice. This paper is an experiment. In it, I consider a worked exercise with the goal of implementing the results of the recent paper. The replication exercise aims at simple code structure that follows closely with the original work, while achieving an efficient usable system. An implicit premise of this exercise is to encourage researchers to consider this method for new results.

1 Introduction

Replication of published results remains a challenging issue in open-source NLP. When a new paper is published with major improvements, it is common for many members of the community to independently reproduce the numbers experimentally, which is often a struggle. Practically this makes it difficult to improve scores, but also importantly it is a pedagogical issue if students cannot reproduce results from scientific publications.

The recent turn towards deep learning has exerbated this issue. New models require extensive hyperparameter tuning and long training times. Small mistakes can cause major issues. Fortunately though, new toolsets have made it possible to write simpler more mathematically declarative code.

In this experimental paper, I propose an exercise in open-source NLP. The goal is to transcribe a recent paper into a simple and understandable form. The document itself is presented as an annotated paper. That is the main document (in different font) is an excerpt of the recent paper "Attention is All You Need" (Vaswani et al., 2017). I add annotation in the form of italicized comments and include code in PyTorch directly in the paper itself.

Note this document itself is presented as a blog post [1] and is completely executable as a notebook. In the spirit of reproducibility this work itself is distilled from the same source with images inline.

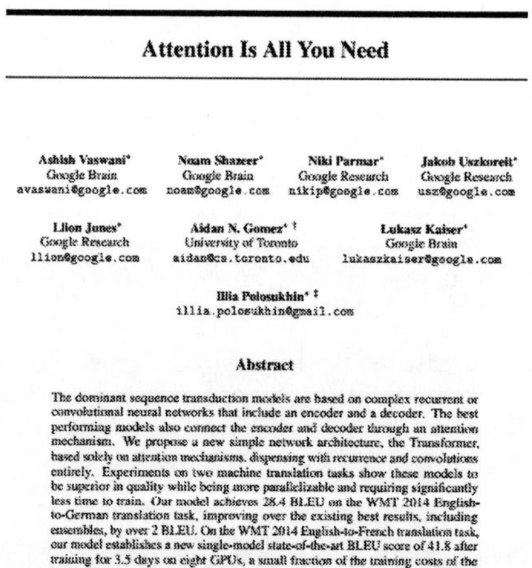

Attention Is All You Need

Ashish Vaswani* Google Brain avaswani@google.com
Noam Shazeer* Google Brain noam@google.com
Niki Parmar* Google Research nikip@google.com
Jakob Uszkoreit* Google Research usz@google.com
Llion Jones* Google Research llion@google.com
Aidan N. Gomez* † University of Toronto aidan@cs.toronto.edu
Łukasz Kaiser* Google Brain lukaszkaiser@google.com
Illia Polosukhin* ‡ illia.polosukhin@gmail.com

Abstract

The dominant sequence transduction models are based on complex recurrent or convolutional neural networks that include an encoder and a decoder. The best performing models also connect the encoder and decoder through an attention mechanism. We propose a new simple network architecture, the Transformer, based solely on attention mechanisms, dispensing with recurrence and convolutions entirely. Experiments on two machine translation tasks show these models to be superior in quality while being more parallelizable and requiring significantly less time to train. Our model achieves 28.4 BLEU on the WMT 2014 English-to-German translation task, improving over the existing best results, including ensembles, by over 2 BLEU. On the WMT 2014 English-to-French translation task, our model establishes a new single-model state-of-the-art BLEU score of 41.8 after training for 3.5 days on eight GPUs, a small fraction of the training costs of the best models from the literature. We show that the Transformer generalizes well to other tasks by applying it successfully to English constituency parsing both with large and limited training data.

[1] Presented at `http://nlp.seas.harvard.edu/2018/04/03/attention.html` with source code at `https://github.com/harvardnlp/annotated-transformer`

Proceedings of Workshop for NLP Open Source Software, pages 52–60
Melbourne, Australia, July 20, 2018.

2 Background

The goal of reducing sequential computation also forms the foundation of the Extended Neural GPU, ByteNet and ConvS2S, all of which use convolutional neural networks as basic building block, computing hidden representations in parallel for all input and output positions. In these models, the number of operations required to relate signals from two arbitrary input or output positions grows in the distance between positions, linearly for ConvS2S and logarithmically for ByteNet. This makes it more difficult to learn dependencies between distant positions. In the Transformer this is reduced to a constant number of operations, albeit at the cost of reduced effective resolution due to averaging attention-weighted positions, an effect we counteract with Multi-Head Attention.

Self-attention, sometimes called intra-attention is an attention mechanism relating different positions of a single sequence in order to compute a representation of the sequence. Self-attention has been used successfully in a variety of tasks including reading comprehension, abstractive summarization, textual entailment and learning task-independent sentence representations. End-to-end memory networks are based on a recurrent attention mechanism instead of sequencealigned recurrence and have been shown to perform well on simple-language question answering and language modeling tasks.

To the best of our knowledge, however, the Transformer is the first transduction model relying entirely on self-attention to compute representations of its input and output without using sequence aligned RNNs or convolution.

3 Model Architecture

Most competitive neural sequence transduction models have an encoder-decoder structure (Bahdanau et al., 2014). Here, the encoder maps an input sequence of symbol representations $(x_1, ..., x_n)$ to a sequence of continuous representations $\mathbf{z} = (z_1, ..., z_n)$. Given $\mathbf{z}$, the decoder then generates an output sequence $(y_1, ..., y_m)$ of symbols one element at a time. At each step the model is auto-regressive (Graves, 2013), consuming the previously generated symbols as additional input when generating the next.

```
class EncoderDecoder(nn.Module):
    """
    A standard Encoder-Decoder architecture.
    Base for this and many other models.
    """
    def __init__(self, encoder, decoder, src_embed,
                 tgt_embed, generator):
        super(EncoderDecoder, self).__init__()
        self.encoder = encoder
        self.decoder = decoder
        self.src_embed = src_embed
        self.tgt_embed = tgt_embed
        self.generator = generator

    def forward(self, src, tgt, src_mask, tgt_mask):
        "Take in and process masked src and target sequences."
        return self.decode(self.encode(src, src_mask),
                           src_mask,
                           tgt, tgt_mask)

    def encode(self, src, src_mask):
        return self.encoder(self.src_embed(src), src_mask)

    def decode(self, memory, src_mask, tgt, tgt_mask):
        return self.decoder(self.tgt_embed(tgt), memory,
                            src_mask, tgt_mask)


class Generator(nn.Module):
    "Define standard linear + softmax generation step."
    def __init__(self, d_model, vocab):
        super(Generator, self).__init__()
        self.proj = nn.Linear(d_model, vocab)

    def forward(self, x):
        return F.log_softmax(self.proj(x), dim=-1)
```

The Transformer follows this overall architecture using stacked self-attention and point-wise, fully connected layers for both the encoder and decoder, shown in the left and right halves of Figure 1, respectively.

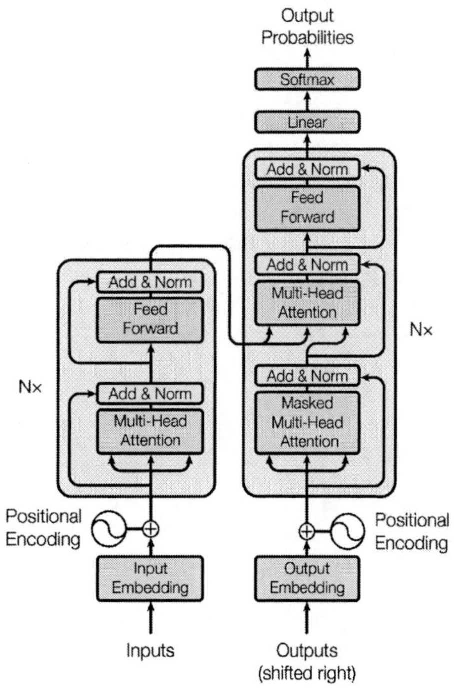

3.1 Encoder and Decoder Stacks

3.1.1 Encoder

The encoder is composed of a stack of $N = 6$ identical layers.

```
def clones(module, N):
    "Produce N identical layers."
    return nn.ModuleList([copy.deepcopy(module)
                          for _ in range(N)])
```

```
class Encoder(nn.Module):
    "Core encoder is a stack of N layers"
    def __init__(self, layer, N):
        super(Encoder, self).__init__()
        self.layers = clones(layer, N)
        self.norm = LayerNorm(layer.size)

    def forward(self, x, mask):
        "Pass the input/mask through each layer in turn."
        for layer in self.layers:
            x = layer(x, mask)
        return self.norm(x)
```

We employ a residual connection (He et al., 2016) around each of the two sub-layers, followed by layer normalization (Ba et al., 2016).

```
class LayerNorm(nn.Module):
    "Construct a layernorm module (See citation for details)."
    def __init__(self, features, eps=1e-6):
        super(LayerNorm, self).__init__()
        self.a_2 = nn.Parameter(torch.ones(features))
        self.b_2 = nn.Parameter(torch.zeros(features))
        self.eps = eps

    def forward(self, x):
        mean = x.mean(-1, keepdim=True)
        std = x.std(-1, keepdim=True)
        return (self.a_2 * (x - mean) /
                (std + self.eps) + self.b_2)
```

That is, the output of each sub-layer is $\mathrm{LayerNorm}(x + \mathrm{Sublayer}(x))$, where $\mathrm{Sublayer}(x)$ is the function implemented by the sub-layer itself. We apply dropout (Srivastava et al., 2014) to the output of each sub-layer, before it is added to the sub-layer input and normalized.

To facilitate these residual connections, all sub-layers in the model, as well as the embedding layers, produce outputs of dimension $d_{\text{model}} = 512$.

```
class SublayerConnection(nn.Module):
    """
    A layer norm followed by a residual connection.
    Note norm is not applied to residual x.
    """
    def __init__(self, size, dropout):
        super(SublayerConnection, self).__init__()
        self.norm = LayerNorm(size)
        self.dropout = nn.Dropout(dropout)

    def forward(self, x, sublayer):
        "Apply residual connection to sublayer fn."
        return x + self.dropout(sublayer(self.norm(x)))
```

Each layer has two sub-layers. The first is a multi-head self-attention mechanism, and the second is a simple, position-wise fully connected feed-forward network.

```
class EncoderLayer(nn.Module):
    "Encoder calls self-attn and feed forward."
    def __init__(self, size, self_attn,
                 feed_forward, dropout):
        super(EncoderLayer, self).__init__()
        self.self_attn = self_attn
        self.feed_forward = feed_forward
        sublayer = SublayerConnection(size, dropout)
        self.sublayer = clones(sublayer, 2)
        self.size = size

    def forward(self, x, mask):
        "Follow Figure 1 (left) for connections."
        x = self.sublayer[0](x, lambda x:
                             self.self_attn(x, x, x, mask))
        return self.sublayer[1](x, self.feed_forward)
```

3.1.2 Decoder

The decoder is also composed of a stack of $N = 6$ identical layers.

```
class Decoder(nn.Module):
    "Generic N layer decoder with masking."
    def __init__(self, layer, N):
        super(Decoder, self).__init__()
        self.layers = clones(layer, N)
        self.norm = LayerNorm(layer.size)

    def forward(self, x, memory, src_mask, tgt_mask):
        for layer in self.layers:
            x = layer(x, memory, src_mask, tgt_mask)
        return self.norm(x)
```

In addition to the two sub-layers in each encoder layer, the decoder inserts a third sub-layer, which performs multi-head attention over the output of the encoder stack. Similar to the encoder, we employ residual connections around each of the sub-layers, followed by layer normalization.

```
class DecoderLayer(nn.Module):
    "Decoder calls self-attn, src-attn, and feed forward."
    def __init__(self, size, self_attn,
                 src_attn, feed_forward, dropout):
        super(DecoderLayer, self).__init__()
        self.self_attn = self_attn
        self.src_attn = src_attn
        self.feed_forward = feed_forward
        sublayer = SublayerConnection(size, dropout)
        self.sublayer = clones(sublayer, 3)
        self.size = size

    def forward(self, x, memory, s_mask, t_mask):
        "Follow Figure 1 (right) for connections."
        m = memory
        x = self.sublayer[0](x, lambda x:
                             self.self_attn(x, x, x, t_mask))
        x = self.sublayer[1](x, lambda x:
                             self.src_attn(x, m, m, s_mask))
        return self.sublayer[2](x, self.feed_forward)
```

We also modify the self-attention sub-layer in the decoder stack to prevent positions from attending to subsequent positions. This masking, combined with fact that the output embeddings are offset by one position, ensures that the predictions for position i can depend only on the known outputs at positions less than i.

```
def subsequent_mask(size):
    "Mask out subsequent positions."
    attn_shape = (1, size, size)
    subsequent_mask = np.triu(np.ones(attn_shape), k=1)
    return torch.from_numpy(
        subsequent_mask.astype('uint8')) == 0
```

3.1.3 Attention

An attention function can be described as mapping a query and a set of key-value pairs to an output, where the query, keys, values, and output are all vectors. The output is computed as a weighted sum of the values, where the weight assigned to each value is computed by a compatibility function of the query with the corresponding key.

We call our particular attention "Scaled Dot-Product Attention". The input consists of queries and keys of dimension d_k, and values of dimension d_v. We compute the dot products of the query with all keys, divide each by $\sqrt{d_k}$, and apply a softmax function to obtain the weights on the values.

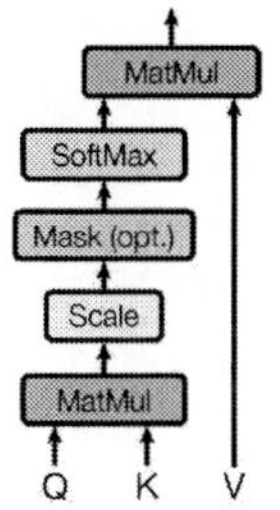

In practice, we compute the attention function on a set of queries simultaneously, packed together into a matrix Q. The keys and values are also packed together into matrices K and V. We compute the matrix of outputs as:

$$\text{Attention}(Q, K, V) = \text{softmax}(\frac{QK^T}{\sqrt{d_k}})V$$

```
def attention(query, key, value, mask=None, dropout=None):
    "Compute 'Scaled Dot Product Attention'"
    d_k = query.size(-1)
    key_t = key.transpose(-2, -1)
    scores = torch.matmul(query, key_t) / math.sqrt(d_k)
    if mask is not None:
        scores = scores.masked_fill(mask == 0, -1e9)
    p_attn = F.softmax(scores, dim=-1)
    if dropout is not None:
        p_attn = dropout(p_attn)
    return torch.matmul(p_attn, value), p_attn
```

The two most commonly used attention functions are additive attention (Bahdanau et al., 2014), and dot-product (multiplicative) attention. Dot-product attention is identical to our algorithm, except for the scaling factor of $\frac{1}{\sqrt{d_k}}$. Additive attention computes the compatibility function using a feed-forward network with a single hidden layer. While the two are similar in theoretical complexity, dot-product attention is much faster and more space-efficient in practice, since it can be implemented using highly optimized matrix multiplication code.

While for small values of d_k the two mechanisms perform similarly, additive attention outperforms dot product attention without scaling for larger values of d_k (Britz et al., 2017). We suspect that for large values of d_k, the dot products grow large in magnitude, pushing the softmax function into regions where it has extremely small gradients (To illustrate why the dot products get large, assume that the components of q and k are independent random variables with mean 0 and variance 1. Then their dot product, $q \cdot k = \sum_{i=1}^{d_k} q_i k_i$, has mean 0 and variance d_k.). To counteract this effect, we scale the dot products by $\frac{1}{\sqrt{d_k}}$.

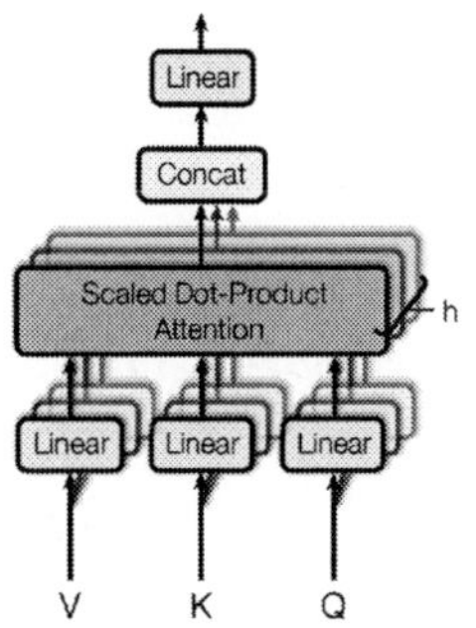

Multi-head attention allows the model to jointly attend to information from different representation subspaces at different positions. With a single attention head, averaging inhibits this.

$$\text{MultiHead}(Q, K, V) = \text{Concat}(\text{head}_1, ..., \text{head}_h)W^O$$

$$\text{where head}_i = \text{Attention}(QW_i^Q, KW_i^K, VW_i^V)$$

Where the projections are parameter matrices $W_i^Q \in \mathbb{R}^{d_{\text{model}} \times d_k}$, $W_i^K \in \mathbb{R}^{d_{\text{model}} \times d_k}$, $W_i^V \in \mathbb{R}^{d_{\text{model}} \times d_v}$ and $W^O \in \mathbb{R}^{hd_v \times d_{\text{model}}}$. In this work we employ $h = 8$ parallel attention layers, or heads. For each of these we use $d_k = d_v = d_{\text{model}}/h = 64$. Due to the reduced dimension of each head, the total computational cost is similar to that of single-head attention with full dimensionality.

```
class MultiHeadedAttention(nn.Module):
    def __init__(self, h, d_model, dropout=0.1):
        "Take in model size and number of heads."
        super(MultiHeadedAttention, self).__init__()
        assert d_model % h == 0
        # We assume d_v always equals d_k
        self.d_k = d_model // h
        self.h = h
        self.linears = clones(nn.Linear(d_model, d_model), 4)
        self.attn = None
        self.dropout = nn.Dropout(p=dropout)

    def forward(self, query, key, value, mask=None):
        "Implements Figure 2"
        if mask is not None:
            # Same mask applied to all h heads.
            mask = mask.unsqueeze(1)
        nb = query.size(0)

        # 1) Do all the linear projections in batch from d_model => h x d_k
        query, key, value = [
            l(x).view(nb, -1, self.h, self.d_k).transpose(1, 2)
            for l, x in zip(self.linears, (query, key, value))]

        # 2) Apply attention on all the projected vectors in batch
        x, self.attn = attention(query, key, value, mask=mask,
                                 dropout=self.dropout)

        # 3) "Concat" using a view and apply a final linear.
        x = x.transpose(1, 2).contiguous().view(
            nb, -1, self.h * self.d_k)
        return self.linears[-1](x)
```

3.2 Position-wise Feed-Forward Networks

In addition to attention sub-layers, each of the layers in our encoder and decoder contains a fully connected feed-forward network, which is applied to each position separately and identically. This consists of two linear transformations with a ReLU activation in between.

$$\mathrm{FFN}(x) = \max(0, xW_1 + b_1)W_2 + b_2$$

While the linear transformations are the same across different positions, they use different parameters from layer to layer. Another way of describing this is as two convolutions with kernel size 1. The dimensionality of input and output is $d_{\text{model}} = 512$, and the inner-layer has dimensionality $d_{ff} = 2048$.

```
class PositionwiseFeedForward(nn.Module):
    "Implements FFN equation."
    def __init__(self, d_model, d_ff, dropout=0.1):
        super(PositionwiseFeedForward, self).__init__()
        self.w_1 = nn.Linear(d_model, d_ff)
        self.w_2 = nn.Linear(d_ff, d_model)
        self.dropout = nn.Dropout(dropout)

    def forward(self, x):
        return self.w_2(self.dropout(F.relu(self.w_1(x))))
```

3.3 Embeddings and Softmax

Similarly to other sequence transduction models, we use learned embeddings to convert the input tokens and output tokens to vectors of dimension d_{model}. We also use the usual learned linear transformation and softmax function to convert the decoder output to predicted next-token probabilities. In our model, we share the same weight matrix between the two embedding layers and the pre-softmax linear transformation, similar to (Press and Wolf, 2016). In the embedding layers, we multiply those weights by $\sqrt{d_{\text{model}}}$.

```
class Embeddings(nn.Module):
    def __init__(self, d_model, vocab):
        super(Embeddings, self).__init__()
        self.lut = nn.Embedding(vocab, d_model)
        self.d_model = d_model

    def forward(self, x):
        return self.lut(x) * math.sqrt(self.d_model)
```

3.4 Positional Encoding

Since our model contains no recurrence and no convolution, in order for the model to make use of the order of the sequence, we must inject some information about the relative or absolute position of the tokens in the sequence. To this end, we add "positional encodings" to the input embeddings at the bottoms of the encoder and decoder stacks. The positional encodings have the same dimension d_{model} as the embeddings, so that the two can be summed. There are many choices of positional encodings, learned and fixed (Gehring et al., 2017).

In this work, we use sine and cosine functions of different frequencies:

$$PE_{(pos,2i)} = sin(pos/10000^{2i/d_{\text{model}}})$$

$$PE_{(pos,2i+1)} = cos(pos/10000^{2i/d_{\text{model}}})$$

where pos is the position and i is the dimension. That is, each dimension of the positional encoding corresponds to a sinusoid. The wavelengths form a geometric progression from 2π to $10000 \cdot 2\pi$. We chose this function because we hypothesized it would allow the model to easily learn to attend by relative positions, since for any fixed offset k, PE_{pos+k} can be represented as a linear function of PE_{pos}.

In addition, we apply dropout to the sums of the embeddings and the positional encodings in both the encoder and decoder stacks. For the base model, we use a rate of $P_{drop} = 0.1$.

```
class PositionalEncoding(nn.Module):
    "Implement the PE function."
    def __init__(self, d_model, dropout, max_len=5000):
        super(PositionalEncoding, self).__init__()
        self.dropout = nn.Dropout(p=dropout)

        # Compute the positional encodings once in log space.
        pe = torch.zeros(max_len, d_model)
        position = torch.arange(0, max_len).unsqueeze(1)
        div_term = torch.exp(torch.arange(0, d_model, 2) *
                             -(math.log(10000.0) / d_model))
        pe[:, 0::2] = torch.sin(position * div_term)
        pe[:, 1::2] = torch.cos(position * div_term)
        pe = pe.unsqueeze(0)
        self.register_buffer('pe', pe)

    def forward(self, x):
        x = x + Variable(self.pe[:, :x.size(1)],
                         requires_grad=False)
        return self.dropout(x)
```

```
plt.figure(figsize=(15, 5))
pe = PositionalEncoding(20, 0)
y = pe.forward(Variable(torch.zeros(1, 100, 20)))
plt.plot(np.arange(100), y[0, :, 4:8].data.numpy())
plt.legend(["dim %d" % p for p in [4, 5, 6, 7]])
None
```

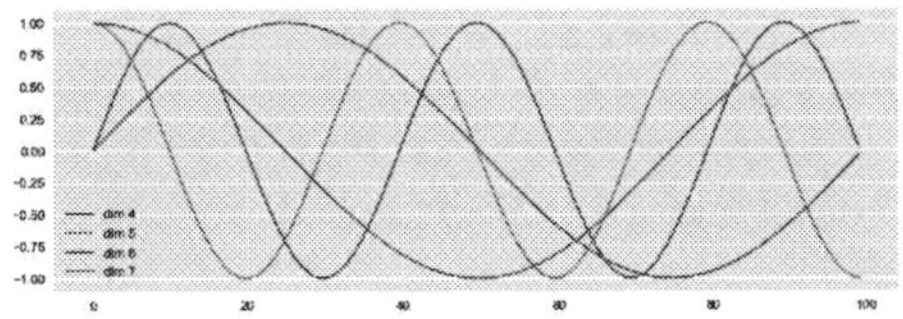

We also experimented with using learned positional embeddings (Gehring et al., 2017) instead, and found that the two versions produced nearly identical results. We chose the sinusoidal version because it may allow the model to extrapolate to sequence lengths longer than the ones encountered during training.

```
def make_model(src_vocab, tgt_vocab, N=6,
               d_model=512, d_ff=2048, h=8, dropout=0.1):
    "Helper: Construct a model from hyperparameters."
    c = copy.deepcopy
    attn = MultiHeadedAttention(h, d_model)
    ff = PositionwiseFeedForward(d_model, d_ff, dropout)
    position = PositionalEncoding(d_model, dropout)
    d = d_model
    model = EncoderDecoder(
        Encoder(EncoderLayer(d, c(attn), c(ff), dropout), N),
        Decoder(DecoderLayer(d, c(attn), c(attn),
                             c(ff), dropout), N),
        nn.Sequential(Embeddings(d, src_vocab), c(position)),
        nn.Sequential(Embeddings(d, tgt_vocab), c(position)),
        Generator(d_model, tgt_vocab))
    # This was important from their code.
    # Initialize parameters with Glorot / fan_avg.
    for p in model.parameters():
        if p.dim() > 1:
            nn.init.xavier_uniform(p)
    return model
```

4 Training

This section describes the training regime for our models.

4.1 Batches and Masking

```
class Batch:
    "Batch of data with mask for training."
    def __init__(self, src, trg=None, pad=0):
        self.src = src
        self.src_mask = (src != pad).unsqueeze(-2)
        if trg is not None:
            self.trg = trg[:, :-1]
            self.trg_y = trg[:, 1:]
            self.trg_mask = self.make_std_mask(self.trg, pad)
            self.ntokens = (self.trg_y != pad).data.sum()

    @staticmethod
    def make_std_mask(tgt, pad):
        "Create a mask to hide padding and future words."
        tgt_mask = (tgt != pad).unsqueeze(-2)
        tgt_mask = tgt_mask & Variable(
            subsequent_mask(tgt.size(-1))
            .type_as(tgt_mask.data))
        return tgt_mask
```

4.2 Training Loop

```
def run_epoch(data_iter, model, loss_compute):
    "Standard Training and Logging Function"
    start = time.time()
    total_tokens = 0
    total_loss = 0
    tokens = 0
    for i, batch in enumerate(data_iter):
        out = model.forward(batch.src, batch.trg,
                            batch.src_mask, batch.trg_mask)
        loss = loss_compute(out, batch.trg_y, batch.ntokens)
        total_loss += loss
        total_tokens += batch.ntokens
        tokens += batch.ntokens
        if i % 50 == 1:
            elapsed = time.time() - start
            print("Epoch Step: %d Loss: %f Tokens / Sec: %f" %
                  (i, loss / batch.ntokens, tokens / elapsed))
            start = time.time()
            tokens = 0
    return total_loss / total_tokens
```

4.3 Training Data and Batching

We trained on the standard WMT 2014 English-German dataset consisting of about 4.5 million sentence pairs. Sentences were encoded using byte-pair encoding, which has a shared source-target vocabulary of about 37000 tokens. For English-French, we used the significantly larger WMT 2014 English-French dataset consisting of 36M sentences and split tokens into a 32000 word-piece vocabulary.

Sentence pairs were batched together by approximate sequence length. Each training batch contained a set of sentence pairs containing approximately 25000 source tokens and 25000 target tokens.

```
global max_src_in_batch, max_tgt_in_batch
def batch_size_fn(new, count, sofar):
    "Calculate total number of tokens + padding."
    global max_src_in_batch, max_tgt_in_batch
    if count == 1:
        max_src_in_batch = 0
        max_tgt_in_batch = 0
    max_src_in_batch = max(max_src_in_batch,
                           len(new.src))
    max_tgt_in_batch = max(max_tgt_in_batch,
                           len(new.trg) + 2)
    src_elements = count * max_src_in_batch
    tgt_elements = count * max_tgt_in_batch
    return max(src_elements, tgt_elements)
```

4.4 Hardware and Schedule

We trained our models on one machine with 8 NVIDIA P100 GPUs. For our base models using the hyperparameters described throughout the paper, each training step took about 0.4 seconds. We trained the base models for a total of 100,000 steps or 12 hours. For our big models, step time was 1.0 seconds. The big models were trained for 300,000 steps (3.5 days).

4.5 Optimizer

We used the Adam optimizer (Kingma and Ba, 2014) with $\beta_1 = 0.9$, $\beta_2 = 0.98$ and $\epsilon = 10^{-9}$. We varied the learning rate over the course of training, according to the formula:

$$lrate = d_{\text{model}}^{-0.5} \cdot$$

$$\min(step\_num^{-0.5}, step\_num \cdot warmup\_steps^{-1.5})$$

This corresponds to increasing the learning rate linearly for the first $warmup\_steps$ training steps, and decreasing it thereafter proportionally to the inverse square root of the step number. We used $warmup\_steps = 4000$.

```
class NoamOpt:
    "Optim wrapper that implements rate."
    def __init__(self, model_size, factor,
                 warmup, optimizer):
        self.optimizer = optimizer
        self._step = 0
        self.warmup = warmup
        self.factor = factor
        self.model_size = model_size
        self._rate = 0

    def step(self):
        "Update parameters and rate"
        self._step += 1
        rate = self.rate()
        for p in self.optimizer.param_groups:
            p['lr'] = rate
        self._rate = rate
        self.optimizer.step()

    def rate(self, step=None):
        "Implement `lrate` above"
        if step is None:
            step = self._step
        return self.factor * (
            self.model_size ** (-0.5) *
            min(step ** (-0.5), step * self.warmup ** (-1.5)))

def get_std_opt(model):
    return NoamOpt(model.src_embed[0].d_model, 2, 4000,
                   torch.optim.Adam(model.parameters(),
                                    lr=0,
                                    betas=(0.9, 0.98),
                                    eps=1e-9))
```

```
# Three settings of the lrate hyperparameters.
opts = [NoamOpt(512, 1, 4000, None),
        NoamOpt(512, 1, 8000, None),
        NoamOpt(256, 1, 4000, None)]
plt.plot(np.arange(1, 20000), [[opt.rate(i) for opt in opts]
                               for i in range(1, 20000)])
plt.legend(["512:4000", "512:8000", "256:4000"])
None
```

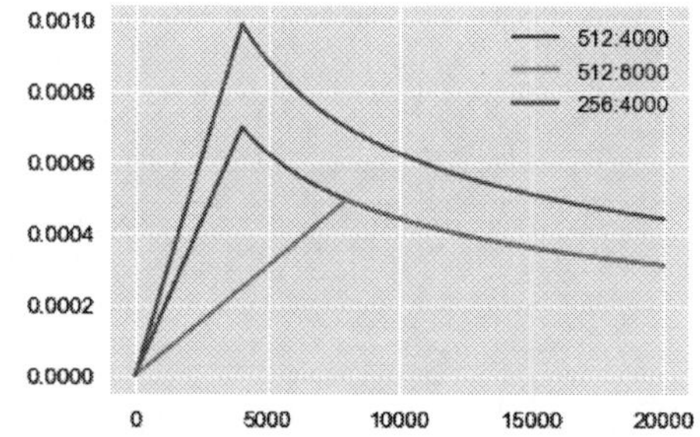

4.6 Regularization

4.6.1 Label Smoothing

During training, we employed label smoothing of value $\epsilon_{ls} = 0.1$ (Szegedy et al., 2015). This hurts perplexity, as the model learns to be more unsure, but improves accuracy and BLEU score.

```
class LabelSmoothing(nn.Module):
    "Implement label smoothing."
    def __init__(self, size, padding_idx, smoothing=0.0):
        super(LabelSmoothing, self).__init__()
        self.criterion = nn.KLDivLoss(size_average=False)
        self.padding_idx = padding_idx
        self.confidence = 1.0 - smoothing
        self.smoothing = smoothing
        self.size = size
        self.true_dist = None

    def forward(self, x, target):
        assert x.size(1) == self.size
        true_dist = x.data.clone()
        true_dist.fill_(self.smoothing / (self.size - 2))
        true_dist.scatter_(1, target.data.unsqueeze(1),
                           self.confidence)
        true_dist[:, self.padding_idx] = 0
        mask = torch.nonzero(target.data == self.padding_idx)
        if mask.dim() > 0:
            true_dist.index_fill_(0, mask.squeeze(), 0.0)
        self.true_dist = true_dist
        return self.criterion(x,
                              Variable(true_dist,
                                       requires_grad=False))
```

```
#Example of label smoothing.
crit = LabelSmoothing(5, 0, 0.4)
predict = torch.FloatTensor(
    [[0, 0.2, 0.7, 0.1, 0],
     [0, 0.2, 0.7, 0.1, 0],
     [0, 0.2, 0.7, 0.1, 0]])
v = crit(Variable(predict.log()),
         Variable(torch.LongTensor([2, 1, 0])))

# Show the target distributions expected by the system.
plt.imshow(crit.true_dist)
None
```

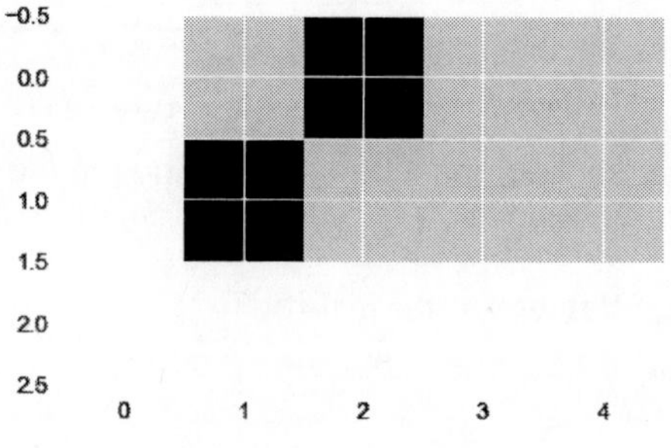

```
crit = LabelSmoothing(5, 0, 0.1)
def loss(x):
    d = x + 3 * 1
    predict = torch.FloatTensor([[0, x / d, 1 / d,
                                  1 / d, 1 / d]])
    return crit(Variable(predict.log()),
                Variable(torch.LongTensor([1]))).data[0]
plt.plot(np.arange(1, 100),
         [loss(x) for x in range(1, 100)])
None
```

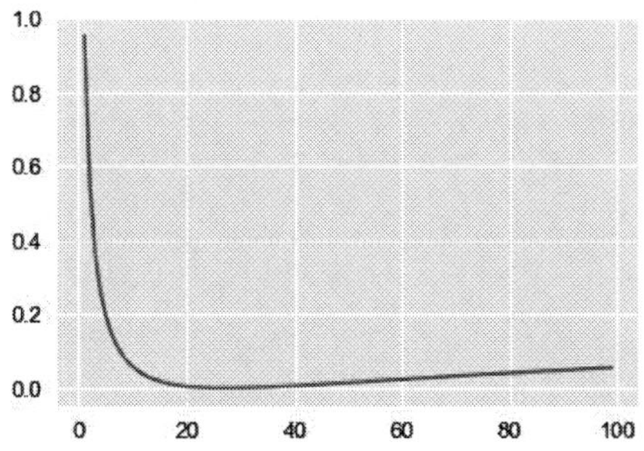

4.7 Loss Computation

```
class SimpleLossCompute:
    "A simple loss compute and train function."
    def __init__(self, generator,
                 criterion, opt=None):
        self.generator = generator
        self.criterion = criterion
        self.opt = opt

    def __call__(self, x, y, norm):
        x = self.generator(x)
        loss = self.criterion(
            x.contiguous().view(-1, x.size(-1)),
            y.contiguous().view(-1)) / norm
        loss.backward()
        if self.opt is not None:
            self.opt.step()
            self.opt.optimizer.zero_grad()
        return loss.data[0] * norm
```

5 Decoding and Visualization

5.1 Greedy Decoding

```
def greedy_decode(model, src, src_mask,
                  max_len, start_sym):
    memory = model.encode(src, src_mask)
    ys = torch.ones(1, 1).fill_(start_sym).type_as(src.data)
    for i in range(max_len - 1):
        out = model.decode(memory, src_mask,
                           Variable(ys),
                           Variable(
                               subsequent_mask(ys.size(1))
                               .type_as(src.data)))
        prob = model.generator(out[:, -1])
        _, next_word = torch.max(prob, dim=1)
        next_word = next_word.data[0]
        ys = torch.cat([ys,
                        torch.ones(1, 1)
                        .type_as(src.data)
                        .fill_(next_word)],
                       dim=1)
    return ys
```

```
model.eval()
sent = """@@@The @@@log @@@file @@@can @@@be @@@sent @@@secret ly
          @@@with @@@email @@@or @@@FTP @@@to @@@a @@@specified
          @@@receiver""".split()
src = torch.LongTensor([[SRC.stoi[w] for w in sent]])
src = Variable(src)
src_mask = (src != SRC.stoi["<blank>"]).unsqueeze(-2)
out = greedy_decode(model, src, src_mask,
                    max_len=60,
                    start_symbol=TGT.stoi["<s>"])
print("Translation:", end="\t")
trans = "<s> "
for i in range(1, out.size(1)):
    sym = TGT.itos[out[0, i]]
    if sym == "</s>":
        break
    trans += sym + " "
print(trans)
```

5.2 Attention Visualization

```
tgt_sent = trans.split()
def draw(data, x, y, ax):
    seaborn.heatmap(data,
                    xticklabels=x, square=True,
                    yticklabels=y, vmin=0.0, vmax=1.0,
                    cbar=False, ax=ax)

for layer_num in range(1, 6, 2):
    fig, axs = plt.subplots(1, 4, figsize=(20, 10))
    print("Encoder Layer", layer_num + 1)
    layer = model.encoder.layers[layer_num]
    for h in range(4):
        draw(layer.self_attn.attn[0, h].data,
             sent, sent if h == 0 else [], ax=axs[h])
    plt.show()

for layer_num in range(1, 6, 2):
    fig, axs = plt.subplots(1, 4, figsize=(20, 10))
    print("Decoder Self Layer", layer_num + 1)
    layer = model.decoder.layers[layer_num]
    for h in range(4):
        draw(layer.self_attn.attn[0, h]
             .data[:len(tgt_sent), :len(tgt_sent)],
             tgt_sent, tgt_sent if h == 0 else [], ax=axs[h])
    plt.show()
    print("Decoder Src Layer", layer_num + 1)
    fig, axs = plt.subplots(1, 4, figsize=(20, 10))
    for h in range(4):
        draw(layer.src_attn.attn[0, h].data[
            :len(tgt_sent), :len(sent)],
             sent, tgt_sent if h == 0 else [], ax=axs[h])
    plt.show()
```

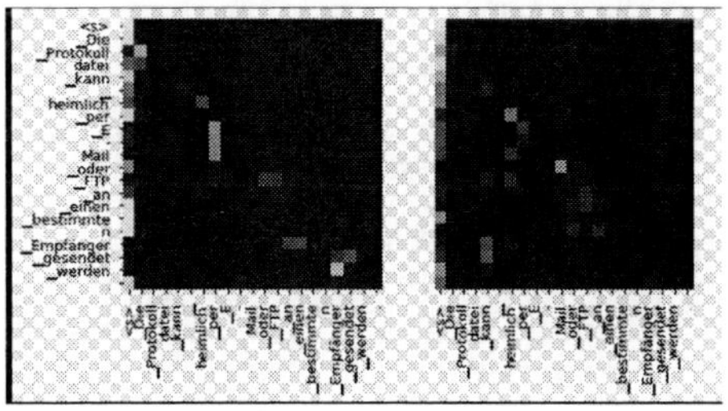

6 Conclusion

This paper presents a replication exercise of the transformer network. Consult the full online version for features such as multi-gpu training, real experiments on full translation problems, and pointers to other extensions such as beam search, sub-word models, and model averaging. The goal is to explore a literate programming experiment of interleaving model replication with formal writing. While not always possible, this modality can be useful for transmitting ideas and encouraging faster open-source uptake. Additionally this method can be an easy way to learn about a model alongside its implementation.

References

Jimmy Lei Ba, Jamie Ryan Kiros, and Geoffrey E Hinton. 2016. Layer normalization. *arXiv preprint arXiv:1607.06450*.

Dzmitry Bahdanau, Kyunghyun Cho, and Yoshua Bengio. 2014. Neural machine translation by jointly learning to align and translate. *CoRR*, abs/1409.0473.

Denny Britz, Anna Goldie, Minh-Thang Luong, and Quoc V. Le. 2017. Massive exploration of neural machine translation architectures. *CoRR*, abs/1703.03906.

Jonas Gehring, Michael Auli, David Grangier, Denis Yarats, and Yann N. Dauphin. 2017. Convolutional sequence to sequence learning. *CoRR*, abs/1705.03122.

Alex Graves. 2013. Generating sequences with recurrent neural networks. *CoRR*, abs/1308.0850.

Kaiming He, Xiangyu Zhang, Shaoqing Ren, and Jian Sun. 2016. Deep residual learning for image recognition. In *Proceedings of the IEEE conference on computer vision and pattern recognition*, pages 770–778.

Diederik P. Kingma and Jimmy Ba. 2014. Adam: A method for stochastic optimization. *CoRR*, abs/1412.6980.

Ofir Press and Lior Wolf. 2016. Using the output embedding to improve language models. *CoRR*, abs/1608.05859.

Nitish Srivastava, Geoffrey Hinton, Alex Krizhevsky, Ilya Sutskever, and Ruslan Salakhutdinov. 2014. Dropout: A simple way to prevent neural networks from overfitting. *The Journal of Machine Learning Research*, 15(1):1929–1958.

Christian Szegedy, Vincent Vanhoucke, Sergey Ioffe, Jonathon Shlens, and Zbigniew Wojna. 2015. Rethinking the inception architecture for computer vision. *CoRR*, abs/1512.00567.

Ashish Vaswani, Noam Shazeer, Niki Parmar, Jakob Uszkoreit, Llion Jones, Aidan N. Gomez, Lukasz Kaiser, and Illia Polosukhin. 2017. Attention is all you need. *CoRR*, abs/1706.03762.

Author Index

Association for Computational Linguistics
209 N. Eighth Street
Stroudsburg, Pennsylvania 18360

CURRAN ASSOCIATES INC.
proceedings.com

ISBN 978-1-5108-6712-3